UNCONDITIONAL BEINGS
LIVING IN A CONDITIONAL WORLD

THE
UNDERLYING
DILEMMA

Dr. Sonya H. Cha, LMFT

MINDSTIR MEDIA

Dedication

I would like to honor this book first and foremost to God through Jesus Christ who saved me from this conditional world. The wisdom bestowed to me was undeserving, and I owe my service to His glory. I thank my husband and four children, who supported me through this journey. My mother, who inspired me to persevere. The rest of my family and in-laws believed in me. My church community and those who have prayed for me and my family. May multitudes find inner healing and encouragement through this book. All stories and examples in this book are fabricated to exemplify theories introduced.

Contents

Synopsis

Many people yearn for acceptance, fulfillment, and satisfaction, willing to do whatever it takes to possess a glimpse of it. It's like our beings are longing for someone/something to fulfill this void. Our ego has a magnetic force that wants to attach to anything or anyone for security. People search for answers, confused by who they are or who they are meant to be. This book provides context to where this dilemma originated and how one can begin to fulfill this yearning in an effective way. Many spend their lives looking for their true identity, not knowing the pathway to it. Are we living as our genuine self, or is it a facade? Despite bad choices or mistakes, one can progress, breaking free from resentment, guilt, and regret. Change begins when understanding the state of one's ego system. Trauma, distress, and disappointments all lead to shrinking the ego system into a cycle of self-negation. Ego Plasticity can expand one's ability to accept and move toward self-approbation. Striving toward a self-approbated ego is key to finding fulfillment and overcoming our weaknesses. Most have circling thoughts of "what if," believing those could bring a happier life, however are they waiting for something that doesn't exist only to lead them back into a negative cycle? The dilemmas we face are due to a lack of understanding of our worldly system and internal makeup of our ego system.

We are **UNCONDITIONAL** beings yearning for sustainable acceptance and happiness yet limited due to our **CONDITIONAL** world. This book will bridge the gap to find the utmost approach toward sustainable happiness as we understand how our unconditional self is integrated in our conditional world. Self-discovery begins with understanding the core of our internal infrastructure being founded on our ego system that has the capacity to expand and change.

Foreword

After reading Unconditional Beings Living in a Conditional World: The Underlying Dilemma, by Dr Sonya Cha, St Augustine's words came to my mind. "You have made us for yourself, O Lord, and our heart is restless until it rests in you." I agree with Dr Cha that our unconditional self will not be satisfied with what the conditional world has to offer. This carries an important message because I see so many people struggling with loving themselves today. The pandemic's isolation environment hasn't helped. Ego, self-acceptance, past trauma, and present conflicts are the game pieces of our daily lives. Dr Cha deals with how to satisfy our soul in the reality of this world. She states, "There's a conflict between our need to be loved unconditionally and the limited support we get from this conditional world." I found myself identifying with many of Dr Cha's stories in her book.

The story of a college student trying to break free from her parents' control stood out to me, growing up obedient and then testing this new "freedom" in college. Even after doing what she thought was living for herself, she is so aware of her parents' disappointment with her. She feels shame, which later adds on to her depression. There is a misunderstanding that "freedom" from parents will bring happiness. Growing up in an Asian family, I have experienced this first hand. Without restoring the conditional love relationship between parents and self, the shame and guilt will affect our ego and self acceptance. Shame and guilt are unduly put upon ourselves from unhealthy relationships with our authority figures and the demands of our culture.

The reader will be able to find their own stories in Dr Cha's examples and case studies. It is a reflective work for anyone who wishes to look deep within themselves to understand self acceptance or lack of. She uses psychological references and also the Bible as her guide in this pursuit. Dr Cha presents the hope of "ego plasticity" and draws the picture of sustainable happiness through achieving balance. I applaud her efforts!

— From Los Angeles, Reverend Tae Kim

I've never seen someone describe how the mind works and how it influences our lives as clearly as Dr. Sonya H. Cha in *The Underlying Dilemma*. In simple terms that anyone can understand and with helpful examples we can all recognize, she puts on a masterclass in how to deal with baggage from our parents or our childhood in order to reach a place of peace and sustainable happiness. How do we balance our needs with our careers and relationships and goals? This book has the answers, and I recommend it to anyone who wants to make improvements to their lives and well-being.

— J.J. Hebert, USA Today Bestselling Author

CHAPTER 1

Self-Approbation

How do we reconcile the discrepancies, differences, and dilemmas in our world? As we see mental health problems on the rise, relationships falling apart, families torn against each other, is resolution possible? It is not uncommon for one to be perplexed by their own choices and actions, living frequently in regret and worry. Feeling stuck in the past, unable to move forward, leading toward a cycle of self-blame, self-neglect, and inability to love oneself. Does this sound familiar? Many have weakened ego systems exhibiting in an external facade, acting in a way that is not true to the genuine self. Where did this start and why? Internalization through trauma and stressors have fabricated an unknown self. Hasn't everyone at one point questioned their existence, identity, and purpose? I believe we need to uncover the underlying issues that are subconsciously sequestered from our consciousness. I will address a quintessence, exiled deep into our subconscious while incognizant of its existence.

Sigmund Freud indicated the ego as part of one's personality, and the Id is associated with primal needs that the ego can navigate (Lapsley & Stey, 2011). Primal needs consume the ego from early on, which are naturally expected to be fulfilled by primary caregivers. The longing for primary caregivers to fulfill all the ego's primal and emotional needs only grows more potent, expects more, and never feels good enough. Although primary caregivers provide their resources, experience, knowledge, and upbringing, they still fall short of total fulfillment consistently for a child. There are many more reasons that caregivers fall short of providing the unconditional love that the child is seeking. This results in a disconnection between the caregiver and child, negatively affecting the child's ego.

The system we live in disallows the ability to connect precisely with the child's interest due to our human nature derived from a fallen world. This fallen world consists of unintentional and intentional parents who inevitably can harm a child's ego at a deeper level. Most parents have their children's best interest at heart; however, children may internalize those actions negatively to their ego state, either at the subconscious or conscious levels. Freud argued that the ego operates at both the subconscious and conscious levels (Freud, S., 2019). The Id navigates unconsciously to engage in need-satisfying pleasure (Lapsley & Stey, 2011). A child's utmost need is simple, unconditional love. When this is not provided, they will go to any lengths to obtain it. In addition, the need for material items significantly increases, such as fun activities or goods. It is easier for parents to provide these material rewards than to make an attempt at unconditional love, quality time, and secure attachment, normally not modeled or taught. Therefore, the Id will eventually attach to whichever satisfying pleasure they can encounter or whine to obtain. Then the ego is shaped and formed based on what is provided by the caregiver and their judgment of the child. Whatever the caregiver believes about the child becomes instilled within the child's ego, shaping the child's identity toward the caregiver's expectations. Ego formation is a critical piece to understanding one's identity.

Ego Formation

The ego is the center of one's identity that drives our behavior and thoughts. The online definition of ego is, "The part of the psychic apparatus that experiences and reacts to the outside world and thus mediates between the primitive drives of the id and the demands of the social and physical environment" (Dictionary.com, n.d.) Our ego is highly influenced by external factors, such as primary caregivers, from an early age. Since birth, there are many extrinsic influences surrounding us with varying levels of stimuli that affect how our ego is shaped. Upon inception, our ego system is not our own and is under multiple controlling factors that are outside of one's genuine self.

Each person pursues their genuine self in varying ways. One end of the spectrum consists of self-neglect, while the other end overtly exerts self at any cost. Many of our underlying needs come from this discrepancy. The genuine self is covered by hurt, fear, scars, neglect, blame, defensiveness, resentfulness, mistrust, and anger. This is called the hidden self, masked by layers of falsehood. Each layer needs to be exposed and healed layer by layer until the true self is revealed. So then how do we discover our genuine self when there are so many layers covering it? The self may not even be aware of what is underneath all those layers. It is like peeling an onion. The more you peel off, the closer you get to the core, and things become clearer and newer. The question is who can help peel your onion accurately? Some seek people close to them, others seek professionals to help find their true self. This journey is not always as simple and easy to encounter, as it involves many variables. Finding the right person/therapist to share it with can be a challenging process. As it may require unearthing painful memories or fearful thoughts that have been avoided for so many years. The fear of negative emotions arising or enduring is also a hindrance. These are all barriers to discovering what lies beneath. First, we must acknowledge that our genuine self can be hidden and undiscovered. This is usually due to our ego formations initiated by caregivers who are imperfect themselves. Secondly, finding a safe and trusted place to unearth these fears, painful memories, negative emotions, trauma, etc. To begin the process of peeling away from the existing self. Many of these fears stay attached to our ego, preventing it from being peeled away and discovered. Therefore, present issues are unable to be addressed when individuals are layered with negativity and falsehood, causing major barriers toward solutions.

A girl lost her mother at a young age and lived with her father and stepmother a few years later. The girl was confused about why her father was with another person, and the last thing she wanted to call her was mom. She grew up feeling distant from both caregivers and internalized anger and resentment for her father bringing in another woman to their home. It seemed he didn't care about her mother anymore. She was scolded most of the time and never felt loved at home. She just wanted to grow up fast and leave home, only to find that she experienced unhealthy relationships, leaving her feeling more abandoned and isolated. She barely made it through college and struggled to financially support herself. Her resentment and anger toward men continued to grow stronger, leaving her no positive image of any male relationships. Just like she felt abandoned by her father, she felt the same way with any of the other men she dated. She felt more alone than ever and decided to receive her own therapy.

Through therapy, she began to discover that all the childhood memories developed faulty belief systems and thought processes that were devastating as each layer was being pulled away. The deeper they went, the more negative emotions surfaced. She didn't realize the depth of internalized anger. It was intensely difficult to express her thoughts and feelings related to her father and mother for leaving her alone in this desolate world. She felt she was disowning them if she acknowledged these negative feelings. However, she learned that she can be angry at the situation and her father's choices yet love him as her biological parent. This freed her from invalid guilt. Some have multiple layers of peeling, some only a few. The peeling process is painful and brings back memories that were hidden for so many years. Through her therapy, she was able to safely share intricate details of how her past compiled layers of resentment, anger, and loneliness. Her hurtful feelings were guarded by fear, tearing at her ego system. This process began to open her capacity to engage socially and perform effectively at work.

Another situation that creates layers of negativity is the loss of someone loved. There are painful memories when losing a loved one. Guilty thoughts, such as "what ifs," "I should have," and self-blame are all tied to the ego in an unhealthy manner causing negative consequences, such as depression or anxiety. To come to a place of equanimity in situations of loss and grief can be a long process that may require a professional therapist. A healthier way to view the loss of a loved one can be to recall the memories as a positive reminder of those times together, creating a ritual of remembrance, and redefining the relationship to a spiritual one rather than ruminating on the guilt and "what ifs."

Grief and sadness are appropriate emotions for the loss that represent the depth of love that should be expressed; however, it is the negative thought processes that increase inappropriate guilt, causing imprisonment in one's own mind. Most people are never ready to peel away at this painful memory. Although everyone needs their own length of time to pass to move forward, one should not be pressured unless one is deteriorating into a depression. There is guilt that prevents one from moving on, believing that they would be forgetting their loved one. In reality moving on means they will not allow such a disaster to bring down two lives, yet one can continue to live by making a difference for others in this challenging world. The two beings can remain attached, a nonphysical relationship can continue to exist. This is one of many ways to perceive a devastating situation, as there are many other helpful ways to view the loss of a loved one. In Christian circles, we celebrate the deceased being home with the Lord in peace and harmony waiting for a future reunion. If the perspective can be shifted, grief may not transition over to depression, which can be easier to manage.

Religion has played a major role in attempts to bridge the gaps of relational disconnections through fundamental principles. I will be speaking from a Christian perspective, utilizing the Bible as a reference. The Bible speaks about an unconditional God that loves his people and is consistent in nature as a forgiving God. God can let go of the past and move forward, making promises in this temporary place called Earth. However, the promises may not come to pass or feel like a decade. Will things work out the way I need in this present world? Many Christians want to believe God's promises are about to change their lives and give them things that they need or get rid of the evil that keeps destroying their lives. There is resentment and misunderstanding when God doesn't answer our prayers or change our situations. Could the issue be that people are searching for fulfillment and completeness in this conditional place?

Fulfillment, acceptance, and love have always been universal needs. Does most of what we strive for in life include one or all of these? If someone had the answer to secure these, would that solve many of our problems? I believe our beings are constructed to be unconditional, yet we live in a conditional system. This creates many discrepancies and impossibilities to bridge the gap. What I mean by unconditional is that one is esteemed despite their external factors such as appearance, race, gender, ethnicity, wealth, accomplishments, religion, job, education, status, skills, etc. According to the Bible, prior to Adam and Eve being exposed to their shame and sin, they were perfectly unconditionally accepted beings that had no shame, sadness, pain, worries, dissensions, guilt, selfishness, and so on. All of this and more came about after Adam and Eve disobeyed God. The fall of mankind is what we call this. Yet our being remained the same, longing and deserving of unconditional love and acceptance just for who we are. The mere fact that a human is worthy without any conditions is what we were created to be, defined as unconditional beings.

From a biblical perspective, the result of the fallen world as sin entered, created limitations, destruction, decay, and temporary happiness (Genesis 3:14-19). Our unconditional self became judged by our conditional world. Our unconditional self attached and grew dependent on our conditional world for acceptance, approval, worth, value, love, happiness, and so on. This dependence grew stronger, leaving our ego at fault with self-blame and self-destruction in the pursuit of happiness. Many allow their unconditional selves to convert to a conditional self to find purpose and adapt to our conditional world. The Bible speaks about sustainable happiness existing within and through an unconditional, loving God. How can this be practically applied in our conditional world? Our unconditional being reaches out to an unconditional God to regain that obscure relationship that was accessible prior to sin entering this world. The unconditional world of no judgment, no shame, no fears, consistent acceptance, and love for one another. The unconditional self longs for this unconditional world. Since we are unconditional beings, this is an innate desire we all carry. The issue is that the world we live in leaves us insecure and confused about our existence. This can be reconciled by connecting with an unconditional God or for those nonreligious connecting with the revolving, unconditional self. Therefore, creating a new self, shifting the ego toward self-approbation is a more realistic way to experience utmost fulfillment given our limited, conditional world.

In Genesis 2:7-25 (Bible) Adam and Eve were created in the Garden of Eden with no shame and a supply of all needs, as life was sufficient with God and His creation. We all seek to go back to this time where no evil, hardships, limitations, guilt, shame, selfishness, jealousy, etc. exist. We have always been and will continue to be unconditional people despite the fall of mankind that limits our situations. Many struggle to bridge this gap. The good news: we are all deserving of unconditional love and regard! The conditions of this world create self-blame or, on the other hand, blaming others. For this very reason, our unconditional self cannot reconcile or manage this discrepancy in this fallen world. We live in a conditional world, where humans naturally judge based on external factors that make up a person. Conditional means one is judged by external factors, and situations are limited because of these conditions. The world we live in has limitations, external factors, and certain criteria in the system that give privilege to one and not to the other. Yet our being deserves equality, grace, and unconditional regard. It is this discrepancy that causes so many of our issues today, especially mental health problems. Below you will see that there is a way one can gain more control to bridge that gap and find more meaning in our lives.

A teenage boy adopted at a young age grows up in a healthy, loving family provided with nurture and financial support but struggles in adulthood with his identity. A void fills his heart with uncertainty about who he is. He pursues ways to feel whole, pondering about his birth parents. One would imagine that wealth, status, materials, and a loving family would bring wholeness to a soul and identity. Yet, there remains a longing for more, never enough to sustain the emptiness of one's soul. Thoughts of why his biological parents would give him up, what was so wrong with him that his parents wouldn't raise him. He contemplates feelings of hate and sorrow, envisaging a search for his parents to find answers. His sense of self is uncertain, chasing to grasp his true identity. His inner longings are so profoundly attached to finding the truth about his biological parent(s) in hopes of fulfilling parts of his missing identity.

Many people may face this common phenomenon when one has lost, been abandoned, abused, or denounced by their primary caregivers. There seems to be a link between one's identity and relationship with the biological parent(s). A void or gap in understanding the self appears when parts of their lives seem missing, forgotten, or dismissed. Our innate nature seeks to be unconditionally loved by our primary caregivers and those around us from birth. Unconditional love is a basic need that is primal from an early age, and the need for it may only increase rather than satisfy. And when we find it, it is temporal, longing for more yet never sustaining satisfaction. Our identity has a fundamental need to be attached by someone or something that provides value, approval, and acceptance.

Indistinctly the biological parent(s) attachment is most often sought out from an early age. When the primary caregivers inadequately provide emotional security, the ego constantly seeks attachment and validation. The ego attaches itself as a magnetic force to elements such as other people, experiences, or materials. It gets drawn to another element to fulfill its gratification and validation. Therefore, many times it is difficult to detach from certain people, experiences, or material things as it provides a sense of security and familiarity. There are times one wants to cease certain choices or behaviors but finds it difficult. This is mainly due to conditioned ways of thinking and feeling throughout the years that the ego has confided in those elements.

The goal is to undo those unhealthy attachments and reattach to new, unfamiliar, uncomfortable, yet healthier elements. When trauma is entwined, the ego can be significantly altered, where one will become isolated or codependent. Codependency can be difficult to end, even when there are negative consequences in the relationship. Stripping the ego away from these elements is like stripping a baby away from the mother's breast after breastfeeding for several years. The distress of this separation is more tormenting than the codependent relationship. Therefore, the ego feels safer to stay in the situation, as the fear of what to do and who they are without this element is more daunting despite its repercussions.

A married woman with two children grew up with parents who separated. This woman vowed not to separate her family. A few years into the marriage, her husband started gambling and spent most of their finances. He kept asking for another chance, and they circled in defeat. The family suffered with barely enough to survive for food and shelter. He then starts drinking and when intoxicated starts screaming and throwing things at her. She is fearful for her life, but she is unable to confide in anyone else for support. Her husband will apologize then repeat his negative behaviors. Her vow to never separate and her dependency on her husband has placed her and her children at risk. Yet the fear of separation is greater than her current situation. Can she ever find the courage to set boundaries and do what is safe for her and her children?

A corporate director grew up with an alcoholic father and depressed mother, being emotionally and physically abused, witnessing domestic violence between parents. She begins to have issues with her relationships, and work increases her feelings of incompetence. She continually strives to prove to others that she is worthy and competent, yet never capable of fulfilling this goal. A compliment from her boss or others telling her how fortunate she is to be a director with a prestigious company is not enough to fulfill her profound void. She strives for more validation, moving up the corporate ladder and having more positive financial outcomes. Yet, it feels like a never-ending well of needs, leaving only uncertainty and fear. She spends her day contemplating how to do better, utilizing all her energy driven by fears of negative judgment from herself and others. Can I continue to stay on top? When will it ever be enough?

A college student grew up obedient and compliant to her helicopter parents' directives and guidance. Once entered college, she wanted to impulsively break free from their care to engage in harmful activities and addictions. All her life, she focused so much on pleasing her parents that she lost her true self. She felt free to live her own life and no longer abide by her parents' expectations and standards. Her family is perplexed by this drastic change and confused about how this could happen. Her grades start slipping, as she cannot focus in class. She lacks the motivation to study, yet finds a way to complete her degree. Her parents are incredibly disappointed in her, and feelings of shame override the well-being of their daughter. Cultural implications with a daughter's education and meeting societal norms become more important than understanding their daughter and supporting her. Parents become more judgmental and bring more shame, adding to her depression. The college student rebels even more, seeing that she will never please her parents no matter what she does. "What is the point? I might as well do what I want." These are just a few examples of what represents the core of the underlying issue, which lies in the ego system.

First, many try to control what they cannot and disregard things that they can control. What I mean by this is that it is easy to blame others or oneself for the conditional world. Why can't I meet those conditions? Why do people have to judge me? This is a system that is anchored and nearly impossible to control. Although people find unconditional regard more difficult to accomplish, it is within an individual's reach. The underlying dilemma to our issues lies in how our unconditional self-responds to the conditional world. Many people see our dilemmas based on the situation or behavior, but these are secondary factors to the real issue. The reason for most of our problems lie in our ego states and their limited capacity. Striving to meet the conditions of the world yet having difficulty forgiving others or inability to love oneself due to these unmet conditions. One can continue to strive to change a world system that is nearly impossible or work toward healing the internal self that can bring lasting change toward fulfillment, acceptance, and love, better known as self-approbation.

What is Self-Approbation?

Self is composed of multiple components with their intricate functioning part depending on the other parts to make it whole. The self is made up of many parts that can be connected, dispersed, or disconnected. Like a puzzle containing separate unique pieces, they all fit together in their natural order to bring completeness. We must figure out the separate parts before we can start uniting the pieces. If you ever tried putting together a 1000-piece puzzle, placing them upright and then aligning them by similar colors begins the discovery process. Misalignment, dislocated pieces, disconnected, upside-down, isolated, and lost or stolen pieces can hinder the compilation toward wholeness. However, it is still possible to continue with some adjustments or gathering them together through positive support and skills. The goal is not to complete the perfect puzzle with every piece in place and in good condition, although that may be ideal. There is hope that the puzzle can exist without all its parts by bringing together the core of what is within that person's capacity and control as the primary purpose.

This process I call Self-Approbation, which is acceptance of oneself, satisfaction with oneself (Dictionary.com, n.d.) Self-approbation allows oneself to make mistakes rather than being consumed by guilt. Many times, we can be our own critics with harsher judgments than others. Regret, resentment, hatred, disappointment, and more can be the center of our identity, leading us into negative thought patterns and unhealthy behaviors. Leaving this negative cycle begins with the process of transitioning toward self-approbation. Other similar meanings related to self-approbation are self-governing, the emancipated self, self-generated, a common factor being a self without an external entity or agent's aid. Self-approbation can lead the self to becoming a more genuine, confident person. It may be unrealistic to expect one to become 100% self-approbated, and is that possible or necessary? Satisfaction can exist like ocean waves, changing in form, inconsistent, unpredictable, external factors affecting the outcomes of where it lands. The self seeks to always find satisfaction, sometimes at all costs. This can result in some displeasure or spouts of happiness only to dissipate and then come back to seeking satisfaction like a never-ending ocean. On a positive note, self-approbation can start at any time, as the self has full control to redirect it back toward self-acceptance.

One must shift toward the concept of self-approbation. Self-compassion and self-regard are also terms that enhance self-approbation. Each of these terms represents a healthier self that allows vulnerability with oneself, trust, internal love versus external love, and the strength to overcome obstacles that come their way. Self-approbation is complete approval of oneself. The question is, whose approval is required? Who is the one person who can consistently judge and affirm the self with full control? Although we may seek approval from those around us, it is not something the self can control. The self is the only person who can control oneself. An exception is in a hostage situation or if the self allows others to take control, then the self is a slave to that person or situation. Someone who takes control of their own judgment and is not submissive to others begins the process of becoming self-approbated.

Self-compassion by Dr. Neff is defined by six categories: self-kindness, self-judgment, sense of common humanity, isolation, mindfulness, and over-identification (Neff et al., 2019). These six categories are measured by one's ability to be compassionate to the self when faced with stress or hardship (Neff et al., 2019). This is the level of resiliency for someone to dismiss negative judgments and move forward from the situation (Neff, K. D., 2016). Stressors or hardship can determine how one responds to self, whether in a punitive manner or with self-compassion. Self-compassion exists when the self can go beyond self-blame and guilt, normalizing the situation by being mindful and kind to the self without negative judgment (Neff et al., 2019). The self naturally goes to self-blame or blaming others when hardship is encountered. However, self-compassion provides grace and forgiveness to the self when necessary (Neff et al., 2019).

There are many studies on various modalities that promote self-approbation, such as self-compassion by Dr. Neff (2016). There are studies that show self-compassion has a positive impact on mental health disorders (Kirby et al., 2017). Self-compassion has been a current intervention in the mental health field as a useful measure for treating psychological symptoms (Neff, 2016). Research has demonstrated that self-compassion is an intervention that has reduced psychological distress and increased well-being through life satisfaction (Luo et al., 2019). Therefore, I conducted a study on whether a relationship exists between levels of self-compassion and intensity levels of anxiety that resulted in a correlated relationship (Cha, 2021). What this means is that as self-compassion increases anxiety decreases and vice versa. This is significant data that emphasizes the importance of measuring levels of one's mental health symptoms prior to treatment and comparing it with their level of self-compassion through a validated instruments such as the SCS-SF and GAD-7 (Cha, 2021). A thorough assessment prior to treatment can guide an applicable intervention to aid in the treatment of mental health disorders. The self-compassion scale short form (Neff, 2016) was utilized as a validated measurement that can be foundational in attaining self-approbation qualities. The self-compassion scale measures self-kindness, self-judgment, common humanity, isolation, mindfulness, and over-identified items in response to stressful situations (Bluth et al., 2017).

Once the level of self-compassion is identified, then one can know whether they have low, moderate, or high self-compassion (Cha, 2021). This is the starting point to determine the baseline of where one stands to move forward. When one can be kind to oneself in the midst of stress, that indicates a healthy ego system to overcome situations. Self-approbation is unconditionally loving oneself despite circumstances, one's decisions, mistakes, errors, failures, and disappointments. Many times, the outcomes of our decisions are not determined until after the fact, while many uncontrollable factors influence the results. Thus, resulting in self-blame, damaging the ego.

An example of this is an employee unsure about a critical decision on a project, and he later realizes his choice resulted in a productivity loss. He spirals into negative thinking, subconsciously blaming himself for everything. Although he made the best choice at that time with the information he had, he still feels responsible. It is his choice to continue down this path and beat himself up for it or understand that his knowledge at that time was all he had to make that decision. Since there were other uncontrollable factors that played a role in the loss. Both paths appear true, yet only one builds and supports the ego as the other one neglects it. The freedom we have is our choice about which path to continue and believe as truth. These truths are relative, since the person believing it chooses it to be true for themselves. While others may see it differently, it is a subjective opinion rather than a universal truth that everyone agrees on. Many times our thoughts and beliefs are fixed, and it feels like it is the absolute, universal truth when in fact it is merely a subjective choice. This is an example of how our subjective truths stem from our frail ego system that has been conditioned to self-neglect.

Self-blame can be viewed as false guilt. The guilt appears real and absolute yet discovers it as false guilt since one is being blamed for something that was not intended nor predictable. In this example, the employee feels guilty for the loss and continues to blame himself, which is false guilt. The reason it is false guilt is due to the employee deciding without the intention of resulting in a productivity loss. If the employee knew that his decision would result in a productivity loss and moved forward with it, then he is guilty. However, since his decision was not ill-intended, and he could not determine the outcome, self-blame was based on invalid/false guilt. Many times, the ego system is impacted by this false guilt that makes it difficult to believe anything positive. Each situation that one encounters as false guilt adds another layer of negativity to the ego system, resulting in self-neglect and self-blame. This thought/belief process can hinder optimal functioning and relationships. Therefore, this process may need to be unearthed to begin the process toward self-approbation.

Self-regard consists of considering one's limitations, desires, interests, capacity, self-awareness, and intentions (Dictionary.com, n.d.) This is similar to self-awareness, where one is clear about their boundaries, how much they can take on, their emotional state, and sensitivities. A self-regarding person takes into account their own abilities and time to support others or to fulfill their own needs. This creates a healthier self to further expand their capacity for others. When one takes care of their own basic needs first, they expand the capacity to support others. It is difficult to support someone else when one's basic needs are not met or have been neglected. The opposite of self-regard would be self-neglect.

Opposition to self-approbation is self-negation. It is common for one to be unaware of their own self-negation. Those unaware find comfort in maintaining a false sense of self or hiding from disclosure of inadequacy. Many are perplexed by their own thought processes and behaviors. I believe the subconscious has more navigating power than our own will, mind, and actions. The issue is that most of us are unaware of what lies within our subconscious that is driving our thought processes, will, and actions. Identifying the underlying issues that lay the foundation for who we are is key to self-approbation. Self-awareness lies deeper than what we can see, hear, or experience. Our subconscious is made up of many variables and influences from childhood to present. Hidden beliefs, thoughts, values, and interests can all be masked from our consciousness. Many suppress painful memories in the hopes that they will dissipate and no longer drive these emotions. The subconscious and conscious can also be in opposition or unaware of what the other is thinking or doing. Self-approbation begins with self-awareness of both the subconscious and conscious areas. Conscious items may be more easily identified, whereas subconscious items may require a therapist to assist in surfacing this area. Reconciling the two can move toward self-approbation.

For example, an adult female is having relationship difficulties and is unable to trust her partners. She would get frequently anxious that her partner would leave her, and no one would be interested in her. She fears loneliness and is unable to feel confident with herself, always consumed by guilt. She seeks comfort through substances and unhealthy sleeping patterns that affect her ability to work. Her relationships are unstable and consistently changing. She finds herself confused about her actions and guilty for not being able to control her substance use. Upon seeking counseling, she finds that her past has influenced many of her negative thought processes of guilt and feelings of blame. Many hidden thoughts were suppressed in her subconscious that needed to be surfaced. This adult female starts unraveling what is driving her thoughts and actions to begin the healing process of change.

There are barriers to unraveling the subconscious with layers of false pretense about the self that may be covered up as the truth. An evaluation of the self, such as the inner self-consciousness is a critical component of addressing the underlying issues. Some find it difficult to view themselves for fear of incompetencies to be revealed or being remembered as a failure. Self-reflection is a difficult thing to do that may require self-acceptance in the process. Therefore, sustaining a false sense of self may be the norm to prevent feelings of inadequacy or ruminating on self-negating thoughts to feed into the depleting ego system. A false sense of self, false belief system, and distorted thoughts may contribute to a negative cycle that only harm one's ego. Many have survived with a depleted ego and rely on other things to get them through; however, crisis or stressful situations can easily shatter these efforts, and therefore further exploration on strengthening the ego is necessary.

Or on the other extreme, the self may be controlled by the pretense self that is made up of lies and fears, unable to give up that destructive control. It is difficult to differentiate between a healthy self, pretense self, and a negative self. When one has lived a certain way, believed certain concepts, all seem the healthy or "normal" way until something greater, better is exposed or experienced. The self can be our worst enemy. It is about which one has more control. The one with more control will override the others. In this case, it is a battle with the three types of self.

The healthy self must win and take full control. Many times, we want to know the "how." We want the answers in a specific order with clear directions to resolve our situation. A quick fix is tempting. However, sustainable change that is long term begins with recognition, awareness, and acknowledgements that identify the "how."

Self-Negligence: "Where did it come from?"

Our history consisted of survival functioning, where the primal, basic needs of shelter, food, and education endured the societal pressures throughout our war-filled history. Previous generations of caregivers were focused on meeting those needs, having limited resources, and lacked experience supporting their children's emotional needs. Previous generations were limited in capacity to provide this basic need. Survival of our basic needs included shelter, food, education, and life itself that was most esteemed. Many have dismissed or been unaware of the basic need to feel worthy and accepted. This can create vulnerability to become an easy target for anyone and anything to fulfill this desire. A lack of this basic need leads to the deprivation that may yearn for a sense of value through unhealthy, self-decaying behaviors, habits, and choices. This perpetuates a negative cycle of self-neglect. Feeling worse than before and experiencing stressors in other areas of our lives can lead the people we love away from us. Subconsciously, self-neglect is a more common and familiar voice that deepens emotional deprivation. One of the concepts of self-neglect involves not taking care of self, placing others before self, and placing self at risk for a more significant gain that may fall short of its reach. When the ego is emotionally deprived, self-neglect may be inevitable due to false beliefs that attending to others' needs above one's own would achieve happiness and acceptance.

A young college student lacks focus and concentration on his career, as he is fixated on ways to help and please others to satisfy his emotional need. He sacrifices his time and money for others yet feels so empty in return since his deeds are not reciprocated. He lives in a cycle of fear that others won't accept him, thus he is unacceptable even to himself. This can become a destructive cycle of emotional pain, making it difficult to attain unconditional regard. Persistent self-neglect can lead to further emotional distress.

A mother who is frequently at the mercy of her adult children fears that their judgment would denounce her worth as a mother, because her value depends on their judgment. Unknowingly, adult children take advantage of her and seek their needs, expecting their mother always to follow through. The mother's fear of being devalued by her children is more frightening than death, because she knows no other value of self than this. The fear of being stripped from the external agents that have placed value and worth on a person increases the authentic self's uncertainty. This can be the cause of repeating self-neglecting behaviors.

A young boy grew up with a mother who was absent and neglected him due to her medical issues, which forced him to grow up independently. His fear of becoming like his mother, medically ill and always bedridden, only increased. He allowed his past trauma to bring fear to his present life. He would always feel that any pain or illness would lead to a terminal disease. He would ensure that he was never ill and worked hard to make sure that he was never lazy. These fears shaped his identity and led to self-neglect. He would not know how to discern healthy boundaries for himself with work, he would always work overtime, and he would continuously fear going to the doctor's office. One may think, "How is this self-neglect?" However, over time these actions began to destroy his relationships, and his physical body could not sustain the amount of work he was performing. He was no longer able to manage his anxiety that increased due to multiple physical symptoms, which eventually caused him to go to ER. This example shows how past trauma can be a significant indicator of self-neglect that needs to be explored.

Self-neglect can also come in the form of pride, overt confidence, and narcissistic characteristics. A man seemingly appears so confident in front of others yet is drenched with anxiety when the attention fades. A couple finds themselves in constant conflict as the husband cannot empathize with his wife when she seeks comfort from him. An executive director is blindsided by her arrogance and limitations to hear and see her subordinates' needs, as those she manages continue to leave their position or demonstrate low performance. A woman of power, status, and wealth is afraid to expose any weakness out of fear that her true self would not measure up to what others expect from her. These examples manifest self-defeating cycles that can lead to psychological distress. Hamsters continue to spin on their wheel in a cage, thinking they will go somewhere better. As the hamster continues to spin in the wheel each day, it is reminded again of this never-ending cycle. Nevertheless, it keeps spinning, hoping for a better result. We all know the wheel will keep spinning in the same place with no other outcome, but the hamster may believe that another outcome is awaiting. Either too scared or unaware of any other options, it chooses what is familiar. Many people live in such a scenario, unaware of their never-ending cycle, leading to persistent indistinguishable outcomes. How do we break away from this cycle of distress and sabotage? Emotional distress can lead to depression, anxiety, paranoia, disassociation, unhealthy habits, substance abuse, addictions, psychosis, and other psychological issues.

Another example of self-neglect seemingly hidden is when the self is given esteem beyond any consideration for others, which can push people away. For example, a man who has guarded his self-esteem by boasting his achievements and success feels the need to be the center of attention to fulfill his void. The desire is never ending and is never enough. He needs more crowds, constant adoration, frequent acknowledgements, and achievements to confirm his success. Yet, each time the need only grows stronger and loneliness digs deeper. How is this self-neglect? The self needs nourishment in a healthier way that is sustainable, consistent, and realistic, yet this man strives to attain it in a manner that expels the genuine emotional need, fearing mistakes and unable to take any responsibility. He would never admit his wrongdoings out of fear of being judged and rejected. Taking responsibility would mean that he was wrong, and his ego would not be able to handle this truth. His emotional maturity is stunted and stagnant, unable to learn and grow from his mistakes due to his enormous fear of being exposed. This fear is so great that it harms those close to him, even his loved ones. Fleeting away into deep loneliness, like a dark cycle of pain that's never ending. To other people he may appear accomplished and sufficient with himself, yet he is one of the loneliest people. Therefore, self-neglect comes in many forms from one extreme to the other. Although the actions appear vastly different, the outcomes are similar and destructive to the self. Understanding the self starts with identifying one's current ego state.

CHAPTER 2

Ego States

There are various types of ego states that are in general the most common. Each one reflects similar characteristics that one may relate to or know of someone they can relate to. These ego states are a reflection of where the underlying issues may stem from or have been altered by external factors.

Self-Neglected Ego: This ego strives to please others at the risk of their own needs, often sacrificing their interests for others. This can lead to depression or anxiety, as the ego is constantly giving out of a dry well and subconsciously expects others to give in return or be appraised. Yet the level of satisfaction is never attained. The ego continues to neglect, being deceived by thoughts of serving others' interests avoids conflict, shame, confrontation, while providing acceptance.

A busy mother with her three children and work is constantly feeling guilty and gives in to neighbor requests to run errands, watch their children, and attend events. Despite her own needs, she begins to avoid her neighbor, hoping not to have to face them. However, as soon as the neighbor is asserting their requests, the guilt takes over and desire to be accepted overwhelms the ego to then again neglect her own needs. She finds herself in a cycle of guilt that takes on tasks beyond her capacities. She continues this to fulfill her ego state that is a never-ending dry well.

Averted/Intolerant Ego: This ego state is sensitive to most things or has a short tolerance to things that affect their ego. This ego prefers to avoid issues and throws things under the rug. This ego is unable to tolerate most people and issues, easily irritated. It has an immense fear of acknowledging one's weakness or error. Therefore, it is safer not to think about it or have it be addressed. It prefers to redirect things to others or pretend there is no issue. This ego wants everyone to stay happy and would do anything to avoid conflict. It only seeks peace and can become overly anxious if things are chaotic, thus trying to escape from it. This ego can feel safe, but the depth of the relationship is shallow, and issues become unmanageable.

A mother who is constantly anxious about her family only wants to discuss positive things with them. Whenever her child or husband confronts issues, she quickly changes the topic or says that is not a big deal, saying to get over it. Her resolution to everything is to cover the issue and ignore it. As issues pile up and the family is unable to have the mother's support, they get frustrated and have difficulty understanding why she is unable to work things out and get them resolved. At the same time, this mother feels safe only when she is able to avoid the issues, as she does not want to experience the immense agony of realizing her flaws or incompetency by resolving the issues. She is protecting her ego by averting all the issues to keep herself safe and peaceful. She needs support to feel safe addressing issues and see that it is not all her fault. Then more peace can come out of brainstorming solutions and effective communication skills.

Fragmented Ego: This ego has parts that are dispersed due to trauma and/or inconsistent attachment figures. Each part is separate from one another, thus always lacking. This ego is unaware of the other missing parts and has difficulty feeling complete. There is a possibility to disassociate or have separate personalities as it acts out from the varied ego parts. There are many limitations due to the dispersed parts that are constantly changing and rarely feel a sense of unison with the self. This self can transition to different personality parts depending on who they are appealing to or which situation they feel is necessary.

A girl grew up being left with babysitters who were physically and sexually abusive. The parents were always working and immersed in their work, so that they did not have the capacity to see the warning signs of abuse. The girl could only disassociate from her reality as the abuse persisted. She felt too threatened to report it to anyone and was left vulnerable to these perpetrators. Her ego began to separate as she was unsure of what to make of her experience. Should she blame her parents? Why did they not know? Did they do this on purpose? Do they not love me? Why would these people do such evil to me, and did I allow it? Did I deserve to have this happen to me? As these questions soared throughout her mind, her ego states separated and had varying explanations and ruminations. Her way of escape was to become someone else or imagine herself to be another character. She acted differently with each person at different times and situations, striving to affirm each of her ego states. Her ego was pulled in multiple ways and required affirmation from various people and activities.

Self-Sabotage/Reckless Ego: This ego lacks self-love, creating habits of self-destruction. Low self-esteem is predominant and will engage in harmful behaviors toward the self, losing any hope in their ego. This ego cares less about what happens to their life and wants to damage it by engaging in impulsive and unhealthy habits. Hopelessness for a better self is inevitable and has already given up on a better self. There is a lack of self-love and more toward self-gratification or temporary fulfillment without any regard to one's future.

An adopted boy growing up with adoptive parents who were emotionally and physically abusive always felt abandoned and neglected. He's unsure of the reasons why his biological parents would abandon him. His adoptive parents treat him worse than a stranger, making him feel a disparity within the household compared to how the other children are treated. He grew up engaging in activities his friends would encourage that were unhealthy choices, but he felt accepted. He began ditching school and getting involved in risky activities. He would get into trouble, yet it didn't matter whether he did good or bad, so why not do what gets him accepted? A deep level of hopelessness formed with his ego that led to persistent reckless behaviors led by impulsive choices, causing detrimental consequences. This ego makes reckless choices with the belief that there is no hope for good.

A male adult grew up without either parent's emotional attachment, searching to feel loved. He finds people abandoning him, turning their backs on him, and taking advantage of him. Through these life experiences, he turns to substance addictions to soothe his emptiness and is conditioned to self-blame. The persistent self-blame leads into a cycle of self-destruction from blame to addiction and back again. This ego lacks motivation for self-improvement and feels hopeless for recovery.

Self-Absorbed Ego: This ego only thinks of him/herself. It lives off self-praise and seeks attention from others. It has difficulty understanding others and can be short-tempered. This ego can only see things to his/her benefit and thrives on enhancing this. Most actions are based on how one can benefit from others or the situation. They only seek their interests and are unable to empathize or take into consideration other's interests. Its primary purpose is to supply his/her own needs. There is limited empathy and compassion for others, as this ego strives to survive on his/her own. Self-praise and self-centeredness are common characteristics one carries, which are necessary to sustain this ego. There is no capacity for others to be part of their ego system. This ego consists of only the self and lives for only the self, which can damage relationships. This ego can go as far as referencing him/herself as a god or one to be worshiped. Although this ego may not see any issues with being self-absorbing, it is a major problem for others around him/her. This ego can be unhealthy, only seeking its own self-interest, which is different from self-love.

A father comes to find his wife and children are distant from him, and he is confused by this. When interviewing the wife and children, they comment that he only thinks about himself and is unable to empathize with them when they have issues or need help. They are perplexed at how he cannot see this. The father has expectations for everyone to adhere to his needs and have them done his way. There is no mutuality, only one way, and that is tiring for them. The family starts growing farther away from him, and even in therapy the father cannot understand their issues. He feels he is doing what he can for them by serving his own interests. There is no capacity to consider others' interests. This ego would need to come to his/her own realization for change.

Self-Approbated Ego: This is the ego that we work to attain. A self-approbated ego has the capacity to consider one's needs first then others. This ego will evaluate whether situations benefit him/her and make a decision based on having a clear self-assessment. They would ask themselves things like: "Do I have the capacity to help this person?" "Am I doing this to please people?" "Am I doing this out of guilt?" "What are the consequences of this decision?" "Will this cause me more anxiety or depression?" This ego protects oneself from being neglected while feeling good about helping others when the capacity is there. It is a balance between the other ego systems listed above. We want to take into consideration our capacities, reasons for decisions, and consequences to avoid self-neglect, yet being considerate to others for the right reason. This can be difficult to attain, as each decision may not be clear and most of the time one must make a decision and learn from them to find that balance. If one is learning from their mistakes or decisions, one is moving toward a more self-approbated ego.

A college student constantly torn between his friends, teachers, family, and his own needs has difficulty finding a balance toward self-approbation. There are demands from people that he is trying to find ways to meet them. He first does a self-assessment, where his priority is being a student, and he needs to attend to those needs first to take care of his ego. Any other demands could come after if there is capacity, such as during breaks or less schoolwork. He would also incorporate self-care activities, such as exercise to reduce his stress and socializing with friends. However, he learns to turn down certain social activities that may cause a detriment to his schoolwork. He is aware of the social groups and what they may expect from him, and he learns to explore the benefits and consequences of his involvement. He would also attend family meetings during breaks as much as he could and feels comfortable turning some down if it means his schoolwork could be jeopardized. He analyzes if some of his decisions are out of guilt or to please others and would learn to say "no" in these cases unless he can say "yes." He also learns to access his support system and weigh the pros and cons of his decisions. He begins to self-affirm and moves away from self-blame. As his confidence increases with building more self-love, he begins to attain more capacity for others.

These ego states can vary in severity along with a combination of multiple ego states. Dealing with a large population consisting of unique cultures, upbringing, response to support system, decision making skills, and reactions to stressors can create a colossal type of ego states. Understanding that the underlying issues stem from the ego state is the start of self-awareness. Self-awareness has been a burgeoning concept that people seek to discover for improvement. However, many people live with little to no self-awareness. Those with limited self-awareness can experience repeated issues and struggles. One may wonder, "How come bad things occur and I keep making the same mistake?" "Why does that always happen to me?" "Why am I becoming like my parents that I vowed never to emulate?" How is self-awareness tied to our repetitious behaviors? A lack of self-awareness makes it difficult to identify solutions. When we fail to understand our ego formation from primitive ages, a negative ego state can deter one from self-awareness. One can go living without any understanding about where their behaviors derived from nor the driving force to make us feel certain ways. A negative self-view or a cover up façade can exist, exemplified as boasting on the outside for others, yet fearful and anxious of being a failure or unaccepted. Many of our underlying fears have to do with rejection, lack of acceptance, and disapproval. Not having accurate knowledge of self-awareness can create falsehoods and negative ego states that lead to repetitive negative behaviors.

For example, an adult son finds himself mirroring the very things that he detested about his mother. She would always be frugal about everything, such as cutting napkins into quarter sizes, saving everything and not throwing anything out, reusing anything possible, and not letting anything go to waste. Growing up, he was so fed up with watching this that when he moved out on his own, he started throwing everything away, wasting away his napkins and any other thing that was disposable. He couldn't stand the sight of saving anything. He feels that his mother was also a hoarder, and he vowed never to become like her. As the years passed, he got married and had a few children. He began to experience the financial pressures. He saw his kids and wife put things to waste and end up buying the same things again and again. He saw himself get so enraged at his family that he told them to stop throwing things away that can be reused. He made sure everyone would wash their plastics and reuse what was necessary for future use. Then he recalled how his mother was the same way, scolding him for wasting things. He was perplexed and confused, "Why should I get so angry at my family when I was doing the same thing and hated my mother for it?" His ego state consisted of anger toward his mother, who would never acknowledge his needs and interests.

Self-awareness in this situation consists of understanding that his irritability toward his family derives from underlying anger toward his mother for not considering his needs growing up and for her frugal behaviors. Anger toward a primary caregiver or family member is difficult to reconcile. This can impede emotional growth, suppressing the negative emotion for possible fulmination at unexpected times and in regretful ways. In most cases he wouldn't be so reactive had he not suppressed his negative feelings from an early age. An excessive reaction may denote unresolved underlying issues sheltered in the subconscious, unrevealed at the conscious level. The healing process for this begins with differentiating the relationship from the behavior. He can love his mother for who she is, yet express anger toward her choices and actions.

Separating these brought freedom for him to express negative emotions about his mother without disowning her. It was not necessary for him to confront his mother directly to share his negative emotions for his own healing process. Since one cannot control the response of another, many situations may be at a disadvantage to directly confront.

When healing one's ego, the self is sufficient. However, a mental health professional is usually required to assist with unearthing this process toward reconciliation. Although people can experience self-awareness on their own, a mental health therapist is highly recommended to improve self-awareness.

What other benefits does self-awareness contain? Self-awareness admits fault, errors, and mistakes in an effort to improve the self, however many are afraid to admit these things due to a frail ego unable to handle the feeling of incompetency. Then one stays stunted in their social-emotional growth, impacting their professional, relational, and social functioning. Years of not addressing areas of self can also lead to medical issues alongside mental health concerns. One is stuck in the past from the time one decides to ignore or cover up one's follies due to fear of how that would define one's ego.

A young boy grew up constantly being told that he was not good enough and was criticized for everything and anything he did by his father. His mother was anxious and would try to control his every decision by telling him what to do constantly. His ego became weaker as he grew older. Whenever he made a mistake, he would instantly cover it up by lying or blaming it on someone else. He did whatever it took to make sure no one knew about his mistakes. Anything as simple as not knowing the answer to a math question to saying the wrong things in front of his peers made him feel "stupid." He vowed that he would never be exposed for his mistakes, so he would find ways to cover it up or redirect the conversation. People would constantly say that he was wrong or get offended by his behaviors, yet he would stay confident that he was not in the wrong. He would lose relationships due to this. Even though people would confront him about his follies, he would never admit to it. He kept this up into his adulthood and now married with children, his family has a hard time relating to him. He would always say he was in the right and blame others. He would also order people around to do the work he was unsure of and then blame them when things went wrong. He would make things up by boasting only about his achievements and knowledge, taking credit for everything that had a positive outcome. Although multiple people would confront his behaviors, he would never admit to it. He was protecting his frail ego by boasting about his accomplishments and taking all the credit for things.

This lack of self-awareness was destroying his relationships and not allowing him to learn from his mistakes, stunting his exponential professional and social-emotional growth. In areas of profession, he was unable to be promoted due to his inability to take risks at work. Socially, he was unable to deepen his relationships and experienced much conflict interpersonally. He is still functioning as that fearful child who vowed never to be criticized by anyone yet doesn't realize that others can see what he is doing and are judging him in a negative way. He continues to make the same mistakes since he was never able to learn from any of them. He is cycling in the same position as a hamster in his cage without any direction or change. Many choose to continue living like this with the consequence of distant relationships as well as lack of professional growth. Some start facing their false fears and address ways they can move toward self-awareness in a safe and trusting environment, through therapy or other helpful resources. Therefore, the key to a healthier self is to understand how one's culture, upbringing, support system, and response to stressors have contributed to developing their ego system.

A professional mental health therapist can assist in exploring this to better understand one's ego state. How does this differ from Maslow's hierarchy? Maslow emphasizes self-actualization at the top of a person's need to be obtained once the other needs have been fulfilled (McLeod, S., 2007). Physiological and safety needs are primal that need to be present before one can even start their own self-discovery. However, self-fulfillment can be obtained whenever one is ready to begin that discovery and start making healthier choices that bring fulfillment, building more supportive relationships and increasing confidence. Although existing support systems are always helpful, a professional therapist can further assist with self-discovery. New or existing relationships are created or enhanced once self-awareness is recognized and recovered. Therefore, the goal is to strive toward a self-approbated ego system.

The big question is how. The answer to this and the agent of change is found on an individual basis. Each person has their own time frame, capacities, and ability to reconstruct their thoughts and ego. It is easier said than done when we are asked to think differently, proclaim positivity, and undo all the conditioned beliefs and trauma. Being conditioned is extremely difficult to change. For some it is not worth it, and they end up living with the consequences that come with it. To reverse conditioned thoughts, beliefs, values, and actions is like changing the brake and accelerator pads learning to drive again or changing the handlebars on a bike that reverse turns in each direction. We drive and ride our bikes without much thought because our bodies and minds are conditioned to the movements that come so naturally. However, if we reverse these critical items, the results of possible accidents, mistakes, frustration, disappointment, hopelessness, and so on could occur due to these changes. For many, it is easier to resort to what is familiar and functions out of the conditioned self. Many of our mental health issues arise from being stuck with familiarity, unable to find enough motivation for change. Positive results are not quick enough, nor do the benefits appear soon enough to motivate one toward a healthier self. Yet staying stuck comes with its own issues that seem redundant, a never-ending cycle of problems.

A young teenager always feels unworthy and blamed for everything that makes her feel incompetent in anything. She is used to thinking ill of herself and easily finding ways to blame herself and put herself down. These beliefs and thought processes continue to damage her ego system and lessen her self-esteem. She is told by others that she is great, smart, considerate, and lovable, however these characteristics do not sound familiar in her vocabulary. Although she makes an effort to think positively about herself, her mind resorts quickly to how unworthy she is. She is unable to get herself out of these conditioned beliefs and thoughts. She is told by a counselor the way to validate herself, but it doesn't seem to work. Especially when situations arise, she is easily triggered and goes straight into her conditioned negative beliefs. These conditioned beliefs have become a primary way of measuring her self-worth. To her it is easier to believe these unhealthy lies than to start believing she is good enough, as it doesn't ring true to her heart and mind. She naturally ruminates on negative thoughts and is no longer interested in positive change nor believes that it exists. There are days she wants change and is tired of her negative thought processes and depression. Yet the challenge to be positive is more fearful and challenging. Life continues in the mundane routine with constant self-blame, negativity, and feelings of worthlessness as she chooses to stay with what is more familiar. Change for this person would require external support to continuously feed positivity to her ego system, since she is unable to give it to herself. She would also need to frequently proclaim positivity out loud despite her disbelief.

Another adult female is having issues with her relationship yet is determined to improve her life. Her conditioned thoughts continue to create barriers for positive change. She tries to have positive self-talk and access her support system, which increases her self-esteem. Although she is constantly reminded of her negative self, she is working on redirecting, replacing, and distracting herself from these thoughts. Although results are not instant, she is determined to overcome these thoughts to improve her relationship, work, and social settings. She seeks out a professional mental health therapist to assist in furthering her goals. As positive change occurs over time, she finds herself naturally beginning to feel that there is some good in her, and she is worthy enough to move on with her life. It is these small steps that aided her to pursue a healthier self, bringing about natural change for the better. For this woman, it was worth the process for change. Over time she was able to repeatedly practice positive self-talk, enhancing her motivation.

What has become familiar is easier to follow than to redirect and change thought patterns. When people meet up with their old friends, are they on guard or concerned about how to behave? Absolutely not, a longtime friend creates familiarity and a bond that becomes a natural part of you. Just like a familiar friend, our negative thoughts become familiar and act like our best friend. It is like going on a hiking trail that has been long walked on. There is no need for direction or expectations due to the nature of familiarity. Familiarity is powerful enough to prevent change. It can come in the forms of comfort, repetition, naturalness, and similarity. Our environment creates and shapes what is familiar as a foundation for our thought process and belief systems. Our thought processes and belief systems are powerful enough to keep us staying on the familiar path, making us reluctant to change paths, or preventing us from trying a new one. Therefore, these self-negating thoughts can become a natural part of one's belief system. They also become one's truth and can be difficult to change. Although you see yourself in a negative way, that feels familiar. These thoughts and beliefs become irreplaceable when familiarity has settled in.

CHAPTER 3

Sustainable Change

How can we start shifting our negative thoughts? When someone comes to your door, what is the first thing you should do? Some will just open the door, some ignore it, some see who it is, some ask who it is while opening the door, and some leave the door open. Ideally, you want to know who is at the door before you decide to open it. Many times, we are so used to opening our door that we don't give much thought to it. Our thoughts are the same way. Depending on how much you allow your negative thoughts to enter, that much more they will take control and invite other negative thoughts to join. Next thing you know, your mind is flooded with negativity. The thoughts have raided your brain, and you are no longer in control, just in submission to them. It is as if someone has hijacked your brain. Ideally, we need to push them all out and shut the door. We may expect them to come back more aggressively, demanding you to open your door or manipulate you. However, you are the only person who can open that door, although it may seem you have lost your rights. These thoughts can easily fool and manipulate to take control.

But our will is stronger than our thoughts if we choose them to be. Some have lost willpower and may need additional support, such as psychotropic medications or other intensive modes of treatment. Some choose to continue in the comfort of these thoughts disguised as their kin. Escape is more horrifying than succumbing to them. When we have found what is familiar and comfortable, change can be resistant. Our nature longs to attach to something or someone familiar rather than meet someone new. Even if it means we could find a more meaningful relationship. Making that move towards positive change, with repetition will transition to a new familiar friend, pathway, and level of comfort. Shifting our thought process is necessary to begin the transition toward a healthier ego.

The Altered Ego

The ego that has been formulated by external factors is defined as the "old self," and the new ego system being redefined is considered the "new self." Trauma, stressful situations, scars from a loved one, or distressing outcomes can all be attributed to internalizing the old self in a negative way. This can build layers of self-neglect, self-hatred, and self-blame. These memories, emotions, thoughts, and feelings often become suppressed in our subconscious, impeding one's life. Some people may continue to live through their repressed subconscious without having their life affected in any way. Therefore, seeking therapy is elicited when our subconscious is exacerbated by a stressor. It is intriguing how our very own ego that belongs to the self and should be controlled only by the self can be influenced, reformed, altered, and controlled by so many external factors. These altercations can also lead to the self turning against self as evidenced by self-blame, self-hate, and self-neglect. How is it that something so crucial to the self can be so frail and susceptible to others, causing potential harm and negative influences?

A fabricated ego can easily adapt to self-neglect. Its strength to overcome conditioned thinking is weakened every time things don't work out as expected. Therefore, the negative self continues to grow, leading to other issues, such as mental health concerns. Most of the time our thoughts are consumed by the "if" and "should" that one is unable to control. These ruminations stall any progress in our lives as they become false hopes. If positive change was to occur through these ruminations, then it is effective, however most of the time it is time and energy wasted, stunting personal growth. There is no benefit from these thoughts if the outcomes are consistently negative. These thoughts can only benefit if one is led to further strategize or plan constructively for these "if" and "should" situations. It is not the actual thought that is so destructive; it is the rumination and false hope that consumes one's life into a spinning negative cycle. Many times, people believe rumination will result in change, yet that is rarely the case. Have you ever tried to repeatedly get someone to do something, yet the outcome stays the same? How much control are you expecting to have over another person who has their own will and interests? Anything over 50% means you are exerting control over something that may not be controllable, thus your methodology needs to change. When one is aiming for 100% control, realism is no longer present, only frustrations and dissensions persist.

We want to transition these "if" and "should" to "want" and "wish." This allows one to be more present with the situation. It sets less expectations, more realistic goals, and enables one to move forward. The change in language can shift one's thought processes from doom to hopefulness. Once negative thoughts are identified, they are flagged then flipped. For example, a teenage girl constantly thought about becoming thinner and prettier like the rest of her peers. Her thoughts began to cycle into intensive inner voices that paralyzed her personal health. She began to engage in binge eating and dieting causing more health issues. Her "should" thoughts had ruminated in her head 24 hours/7 days a week. She had lost control of her thoughts.

As she began to seek therapy, she realized most of her thoughts were defeating and discouraging. They were all too familiar to her, making it difficult to differentiate between them. Her weight and appearance were never enough, although she lost pounds. Once she began learning to flag these thoughts and change them to "I wish I was thinner and prettier," she began to redefine what thinner and prettier entailed, taking small steps toward realistic goals that were attainable. She learned to discard comparison amongst her peers once she realized there was no end to it. She began to feel more in control of her thoughts and easily flagged and flipped her ruminations. The practice of flagging and flipping thoughts was essential for her social emotional growth. When outcomes were not to her benefit, she felt the negative emotion, acknowledged the negative thought, then before it spiraled, she replaced it with a helpful thought. She made an effort to tell herself that she is working on a healthy diet and close to reaching her weight. She set an attainable goal of losing a few pounds in two weeks. For an ego to be strengthened, it must practice flagging and flipping unhealthy ruminations that constantly hinder our progress.

Attachment Beings

Attachment begins from the womb, through familiar people. The attachment continues from birth throughout the lifespan, acquiring comfort from other individuals, concepts, or tangible items. Bowlby indicated that attachment is between oneself and other individuals, particularly primary caregivers that continues throughout adulthood (McLeod, S.A., 2017). Although some may have varying ways of attachment, Bowlby referred to it between individuals (McLeod, S.A., 2017). Primary attachment figures are usually caregivers from birth. We are attachment beings by nature, however the attachment can be other than individuals, such as concepts or materials.

A male adult finds his wife requesting a divorce and is in anguish, begging her to stay. He finds it difficult to separate due to being addicted to the concept of marriage. The person is unable to fathom life without this partner and realizes that it is not so much the person but rather the concept of being with someone that he is intensely attached to. After seeing his own parents' fallen marriage, he became enmeshed with the idea of being in a marriage. He feared being left alone. Later, through therapy, he realized that his marriage was due to the concept of being in a marriage, meeting married couples, going to church with a partner, always having a partner at social outings, and being able to come home knowing that someone was waiting for him. He admitted that he was never really attracted to her nor considerate of her needs, as he would only do things for her if he felt threatened that she would leave him. He lived in anxiety, worrying about her leaving him, and when it finally happened he had a mental breakdown. An ego system can also be attached to material things or addictions to help them feel secure. They become dependent on these things to find sanity. A male adult is uncontrollably into collecting cars, more concerned about the condition of his cars than his own health. He feels a sense of pride and security when he has certain types of cars in his collection. Some people can be significantly attached to their pet. As you can see, our attachment is not always with people. This signifies that we need to find healthy attachments that provide security with minimal consequences. The attachment to external factors can create more anxiety and depression when there is separation. Therefore, alternatives and a multitude of attachment figures may be helpful in these situations. It is not the attachment itself that makes it unhealthy, it is the outcome of what happens when a person is separated from it. A weak ego system can be shattered when their attachment figure is detached. Strengthening one's ego system is critical to avoid these detrimental circumstances.

Need vs. Want

People may believe that deep connections are easily attainable for others. Exposure to social media, successful stories, and other people who present themselves as happy create a pretense that connectedness is attainable. Although there may be some people who believe they have attained this, many continue to seek it. When we seek something that doesn't come easily, we find ourselves negating our ego. Our ego becomes deprived from acceptance, and it feels the absence of deep connections or sustainable happiness due to our unworthiness. As deprivation increases, desperation excels. Acceptance, approval, worthiness, etc. are basic needs to a human soul. When these are obsolete or inadequate, the hunger to attain it grows immensely. One will attain a glimpse of it at any cost. In a situation of a natural disaster, when food is no longer in sight after several days, any food found even if smothered in dirt or in trash will be consumed. This basic need is so crucial for survival that it will create desperation, leaving people impulsively eating whatever they see in sight. Our human nature has basic needs that if unmet, desperation and impulsivity can prevail.

A father, a husband trying so hard to keep his family together, has difficulty controlling his sexual desires. He thrives on the attention of other women, yearning for more whenever the opportunity arises. His powerful status, wealth, and position hail an audience of women whose attention fulfills his void and need for approval. Although he knows he could lose his family and is overwhelmed with guilt, his rationality is no longer powerful enough to overcome his desires. His persistent longings led to physical intimacy with various women. Then he wakes up with regret and guilt, unable to forgive himself. He knows his family is placed on the line, yet the desperation overrides his rational wishes. Through therapy, he realized that the lack of emotional security and love from his mother created a desire for maternal attention. He grew up with a mother who had her own mental health issues that disabled her from connecting in a nurturing way for him. His father left the family at an early age and was never contacted. He knew that he would need to succeed in all aspects to become wealthy and powerful to force attention on himself. He made sure he left his mother once he turned eighteen and moved out to support himself. His basic need for unconditional love was deprived from an early age that he desperately sought attention from others. He grew to succeed in the world to supply his pleasure of attention from women. However, it was never enough, and he wanted more attention, losing control, and destroying his marriage and family. He was left alone, and no number of women could sustain his pleasures. This is an example of how being deprived of acceptance and worth, a basic need, led to desperation for uncontrollable desires that became self-destructive.

Our ego begins to yearn for others acceptance to purvey our value and worth. Our worth becomes dependent on external factors and others to fulfill this need. We want our ego to transition from needing external factors to wanting them. Desiring others' approval is additional support that is not required for the ego to thrive. The ego only needs the self to approve for survival. If you find yourself persistently unacceptable or unworthy, that may indicate codependency on external factors to sustain fulfillment and happiness. One may find that this negative cycle continues with no changes or positive results. Thus, one is focusing on needing external factors to purvey ego satisfaction, which is not sustainable, realistic, nor nourishing to our egos.

Self-approbation's goal is to purvey the ego with positivity through consistent means, such as the self or through one's spirituality. The ego should shy away from needing external factors to purvey fulfillment rather an interest to attain it if provided. For example, when we eat a cake, it is the cake itself that is the main ingredient and the icing along with decorations are additional items that make the cake even more splendid. Although the decorations are missing, the cake is still standing and existent without anything else. Of course, we all want more decorations and icing to taste better and be more presentable. However, its absence does not abate the existence of the cake. The ego stands despite others' approval. As humans we long for relationships, therefore filtering healthy relationships to enhance the ego is optimal for self-improvement. We want to surround ourselves with people who are reciprocal and supportive to enhance our ego. We may have limits to fulfilling this satisfaction as well. Therefore, instead of seeking one person to supply that deep connection, surrounding oneself with multiple supportive people across a time span in smaller increments is more realistic. Spirituality is another part of our being that can be accessed and goes beyond the human limitations. When our spirit is connected to unconditional love, grace, and forgiveness, sustainable happiness and peace can be found.

CHAPTER 4

Spirituality

Most of our focus on wellbeing has been on the mind and body. The soul is another component of the ego that can expand our human limitations and resources. Our soul plays an essential role in finding fulfillment, yet most are unaware of how to tap into their spirit. Some have rejected their spirit due to being harmed by others in religion. Religion is an institute or specific set of beliefs, while spirituality is another part of the self that can benefit the ego, especially when the self is limited or needs to amplify self-love. Our unconditional beings are limited to the conditional systems of this world that hinder our happiness. The negative thought cycles are never ending, unable to be ceased even with treatment. The hurtful past and trauma are unforgettable, unforgivable, conditioned into one's ego system to negate the self and grow in self-hatred or hatred toward the world. These are human limitations that have obstructed the ability for the self to heal. Is there anywhere else to turn to when one is unable to engage in self-love or heal from their past? Can the self abjure conditional thinking and habits?

The soul is the distinct part of our self that is separate from our body (Dictionary.com, n.d.) The soul exists to mend the brokenness between our mind and body when the self is incompetent to do so. This is where one can explore their spirituality in ways to benefit the ego. Our soul is part of a resource that exists to overcome that which we have no control of, such as situations, emotions, and thought processes. Attaching onself to another entity that can provide unconditional love and regard can expand human limitations as it naturally brings peace and hope. Although the situation remains the same, the inner ego finds internal strength to surpass the present stressor. Internal thoughts naturally transition to being constructive, finding peace despite the circumstance. The key to inner healing is not to remove or change the situation/person, rather accessing resources to shift the perspective toward acceptance and solutions. Spirituality can help find ways to cease negative ruminations, especially when human limitations persist.

When one is inclined to access their soul for additional support, each person's journey can be unique. Finding spirituality for each person has its own timing, methods, and resources. Whichever way one pursues this resource, the outcome should reflect unconditional love and regard. This additional support is especially helpful when other supports are insufficient or obsolete. A simple prayer for God to reveal himself can be the beginning as his unconditional love enhances self-love. It is crucial that the outcome of this resource evolves into a self-approbated ego. A spiritual resource should emulate a positive impact in one's life toward unconditional love.

Accessing our spirituality is another resource to sustain happiness more frequently or for longer periods of time. Spirituality can be defined in many ways for various people. It is a part of us that goes beyond human limitations. When emotions are endless, situations out of control, or resources limited, another channel of hope exists. Spirituality can provide a sense of peace amid a storm that is unexplainable. It can shift perspectives in the most gruesome times when our minds are fixated. It can ignite passion and motivation when our conditional world cannot. Spirituality connects us to our inner self outside of this conditional world and into the unconditional world. However, when religion and spiritual groups cause harm and distress then it can be destructive to the inner self. The outcomes of one's spirituality should provide a sense of unconditional love, acceptance, and worth. It should expand and support our ego toward self-approbation. If it is not, then one should seek other means to attain unconditional acceptance.

A young boy growing up was always told he could never become someone, that he always made mistakes. His parents even called him a mistake, criticizing every accomplishment he made. Although he attempted to think positively, the inner voices of his parents' dissatisfaction rang truer. More than forty years of criticism led him to believe these lies, leading him toward self-neglect and self-hatred. After several years of therapy, he was unable to recondition his mind, as his racing thoughts would not cease. He lost control of his thoughts and had difficulty redirecting them. He engaged in multiple treatments and medications, yet these internal thoughts would not disappear. He began to attend a church service he was invited to by his friend. In the beginning, he was triggered when hearing about a loving God that would possibly never love him. Any positive messages would be transitioned to a despairing thought of self-hatred. As people in the church began to pray for him and show him unconditional love, his heart warmed up, enjoying their company. Through their fellowship, he experienced acceptance like never before. He felt wanted and appreciated for the first time. The prayers had a significant impact on his negative thought processes, and he began to feel love for the first time. Although he was unable to change his thoughts and conditioned beliefs, his spirit was able to connect with God. He found himself stretching beyond his human limitations to bring positive change. His soul was revived through his spirit, mending the years of brokenness in his mind and body. For those who are unwilling to tap into their spirituality. It is recommended to seek unconditional love from within. However, when our humanness is limited with no possible solutions, we have access to our spirituality to expand this capacity toward sustainable change and a self-approbated ego. Exploring ways to support our wellbeing through spirituality is a critical resource that can be an agent of change for many.

Our ego system can feel as if it is fixed, unable to be changed or adjusted. This is like clay and ceramic pots. Once dried, it is impossible to change the shape. Clay pots are made from a chunk of clay that twirls on a pottery wheel with hands shaping and molding its figure from its liquid form. Once completed, it dries and hardens, becoming a fixed product that cannot be reshaped unless crushed. This is similar to how our ego is formed through the hands of others. Whether they have good or bad intentions, we don't get to choose who and what will shape our ego from birth. As the hands indulge through the liquid clay, arduously constructing the ego into something they believe is best. They are the people shaping the clay with full control, limiting genuine exposure. Are we all constructs of our caregivers, society, culture, family, and friends? Is it possible to maintain authenticity from birth? Just like a baby is dependent on caregivers to nurture and ensure basic needs, our ego is also dependent on caregivers to construct us as close to our authentic self. Yet, where do these hands come from? These hands have a history of trauma, stress, fears, expectations, perfectionism, cultural beliefs, societal pressures, and the list goes on. The ego formation becomes permeated with all these filters, believing this is who you are and who you will become without any say. Some egos eventually realize what is happening and will rebel, and others driven by self-blame concede to the expectations. A perfect ego does not exist; therefore, we cannot compare or judge others as to which ego is better. We work with identifying our ego state and choose to progressively transition into a healthier one. Our ego yearns for acceptance, approval, validation, and unconditional love, therefore, becomes an attached component to anything that could fulfill this need. Emotional security is a basic need, like hunger, although it is not as visible and noticeable as hunger pains. Hunger pains are more easily experienced and easier to resolve. Emotional security is colluded with other needs and experiences that make it difficult to address.

A child growing up with one parent subconsciously questions, "Where is my other birth parent, and why do other kids have both their parents?" These are inner questions, thoughts, ideas, judgments, beliefs, and rationales that are formulated within the subconscious that may not be noticeable. They accumulate like storage becoming a part of our ego formation. Life situations, events, and relationships foster this formation, but the deeper underlying thought processes are governed by what lies within our subconscious. Most people are unaware of what is underneath in their subconscious, as one only experience what is visible at the conscious level. The external factors, such as outcomes, titles, income, appearance, social networks, living situation, status, power, wealth, commodities, etc. are what measure our ego. Many strive to uphold their utmost potential in these areas. Rarely does one focus or examine what lies within the inner self. Those who meditate and have increased self-awareness tap into both the subconscious and conscious states, having a deeper insight into their own being and care for oneself. Therefore, mindfulness practices and healthy thought processes are important to sustain deeper self-awareness.

How can such a fixed ego system be altered? When it is conditioned since birth, it can feel impossible to change. Our ways of thinking, values, and belief systems become fixed as years pass. Fortunately, our ego is not stamped in stone and fixed like clay pots. It can be refurbished or reconstructed. The old clay pot can be melted or discarded, and a new set of clay can start on the pottery wheel, but which hands can shape and mold a genuine self with controllable factors? Will you allow your family members, friends, society, and culture to continue to be those hands to shape and mold who you are? If so, expect the same results of disappointments, confusion, inconsistency, instability, or wavering, as they are being influenced from another imperfect perspective.

Each person is made up of their own ego that may not be genuine with their own upbringing and past that can affect the way they would influence you. There is only one human being who can provide consistent unconditional positive regard and love. That is the self, which has the most control of one's ego. Although the self can be limited as well, it is the closest one to provide that consistency. However, there are those who have neglected the self, staying stuck in their own negativity. Therefore, the other being that can provide unconditional love and regard more consistently is a higher power, such as God, if one chooses to believe in one. It is especially helpful when the self is incapable of providing unconditional love to their own ego. Therefore, I recommend exploring one's spirituality to assist with this. Many times, we are only conscious of our mind, body, and circumstance, overlooking the spiritual part of ourselves. Some have no interest in exploring their spirituality, nor do they know where to begin. Usually, it takes a stressful situation for spiritual interests to be naturally sparked. Spirituality can support an ego when the self cannot. It can go beyond human limitations and expand capacities to overcome difficult situations. Tapping into spirituality can support the ego, whether limited in capacity or overly supplied with positivity. A multitude of resources that include spirituality and other sources is helpful to be dependent on to enhance the ego. The issues lie when the ego allows external factors with their own limitations to redefine who they are.

Some people have stayed away from religion or recall God as an angry, unloving God that makes it more difficult to depend on for unconditional regard. There has been much hurt and pain due to religion or trauma and fear. In these situations, it may not be helpful to the ego to pursue this unless this has been reconciled. Spirituality can be experienced in one's own time and experience that needs to be supportive to one's ego. I will reference the Christian God through Jesus Christ due to my personal experience that has strengthened my ego to love myself unconditionally. The Christian God is a God of grace and love due to the sacrifice of his only son, Jesus Christ, which became the atonement to open that channel to experience unconditional love and regard. Positive fellowship with other believers, involvement in the Church, personable relationship with Jesus through prayer and other disciplines can ameliorate the ego system toward a genuine, unconditionally loving self as additional resources.

We start this process with a new set of clay on that pottery wheel that is now controlled only by the self. Any judgments are redirected by the self rather than influenced by external factors. As one is shaping and molding their new self, it deflects other's judgments or control by disallowing their presumptions to permeate into one's ego system. Once one can differentiate between the false ego and the new ego, it can be fostered and redefined by the unconditionally loving self. Developing a new ego can provide more security, accuracy, sustainability, positivity, consistency, and validity. These are attributes that most people long for and strive to reach, however due to an unhealthy ego system these goals rarely get met. Our ego is adaptable and can change in format as we redirect our thoughts and shift our previous belief systems that may have been more harmful than helpful. This process is referred to as ego plasticity. Similar to neuroplasticity, ego plasticity can transition out of the conditioned place into a new way of perceiving one's ego that is exceptionally healthier and beneficial to the individual (Puderbaugh, M., & Emmady, P. D., 2022). It requires relentless redirection of negative thought processes, changes in belief systems causing a negative impact, and persistent self-affirmations/self-compassion practices.

CHAPTER 5

Ego Plasticity

Ego plasticity can adjust our perspective, thus leading to changes in behaviors. Initially our ego is shaped through others and various external factors, therefore it requires self-awareness and self-assessment to work toward ego transformation. How does ego transformation work? First, discarding one's previous self traits that caused unfavorable outcomes then identifying positive traits worth treasuring to retain with the new self. The focus of new self and ego transformation lies on what is current and what is ahead that is beneficial to the self. This is done by relinquishing a negative ego system toward an affirmative ego consisting of self-affirmations, self-compassion, and self-approbation. Many times, we think others and external factors are the only thing that can fulfill our longing to be accepted and valued. The good news is that the self can fulfill this need in a sustainable, unconditional, and consistent manner. Since it is controlled by the self, these can remain consistent.

When our ego is influenced by others, there exists inconsistency, unsustainability, and uncertainty. Many times, one looks to others to provide that affirmation, appreciation, and acknowledgement. However, sometimes it is never enough, or the person we hope to provide this disappoints us. Therefore, we live in a conditional world that indefinitely inculcates our ego with acceptance being validated through external factors. Common external factors people seek value from are our parents, partners, bosses, co-workers, social media, professors, family members, children, and so forth. When this is unfulfilled, our ego either self-neglects, self-blames, or blames others. Is it accurate to say that one's value is unworthy when an external factor does not affirm it? There may be multiple reasons, such as their own perceptions or upbringing clouding their judgment and actions, lack of capacity for others, or other motives that disable one to affirm. Whatever the reason, it is rarely associated with one's self worth, yet our own ego naturally assumes negativity and displaced judgment.

An adult female lived a normal life growing up, so she thought, until she began to have anxiety attacks as an adult. She was paralyzed when it came to leaving her home or engaging with people, she was not familiar with. Her anxiety prevented her from working, and therefore she lived with her mom. Throughout therapy, she had difficulty managing her anxiety even with medication support. The therapist explored her earlier years to unearth layers of self-neglect that may be impacting her anxiety. Her parents had divorced at an early age and didn't have enough emotional capacity to nourish her ego. She would be taken back and forth, without much stability and ended up being cared for by her maternal grandmother. The constant changes, unstable living situations added layers of self-blame. Internally she began to blame herself for her parents' separation, being tossed back and forth from home to home. She discovered that all her life she was blaming herself for her parents' lack of emotional security and divorce. She was displacing her parent's responsibility to herself. Displacement is when one is misplacing responsibility or negative emotion to an inappropriate person, usually the self. There is a responsibility that exists, yet who and how much responsibility can vary.

She was subconsciously blaming herself for her parent's decision to separate and the unstable living situation that laid the foundation for her anxiety. She felt too guilty to blame her parents for her past. Once she understood that it was her parents' decision to separate, and they did not have the emotional capacity nor knowledge of how to nurture her, she was able to find acceptance. Her anger toward the self was also displaced, therefore she allowed herself to redirect her anger at the appropriate person/situation. Once she began expressing her anger toward divorce, she began to free herself from covered layers of self-blame. She drew a pie chart and divided the responsibility of her parent's separation, 50% for each parent and her responsibility was left at 0%. Whereas prior to therapy, it was 100% her responsibility along with 100% anger was directed at the self. She felt more comfortable blaming the situation than her parents to reduce the guilt. When displacement is on the self, it takes on others' responsibility that weighs down their ego, making it more difficult to self-love. These are additional layers that need to be uncovered and removed to support self-approbation.

Ego plasticity allows one to reshape and remold the damaged self to something more positive, bringing hope to one's self-esteem. Identifying characteristics that are positive and ones to acquire or admire in others is a start toward a healthier new self. Constant redirection and replacing negative thought processes are part of the journey toward self-approbation. Repetition of positive self-affirmations is also required to rewire the conditioned self toward a positive ego. Self-approbation is defined as "satisfaction with oneself or self-approval" (Dictionary.com, n.d.) Many of our inner battles result in lack of self-satisfaction/self-approval. It is easier said than done to rewire an ego system that has been conditioned and set to think, act, and behave in a certain way. A therapist can assist in identifying ways one is conditioned to think, act, and behave to analyze how it is being impacted mentally. This exploration process of the self is helpful to start toward attaining self-approbation. Self-approbation starts with self-awareness. Without self-awareness, it is difficult to know where to start and what issues exist that created barriers toward progress.

Assess, Awareness, Acceptance, and Action are the four steps to reverse conditioned thinking. The first step is to assess the issues, negative thoughts, and how one has been conditioned. What are the current issues and negative thought processes that have been conditioned? One must consider reflecting on past stressors or trauma to identify the connections to current issues. The stressors can easily be internalized at the subconscious level, impacting the ego without awareness of one's consciousness. For example, a child growing up witnessing his parents argue and fight often begins to normalize the situation that peace between a couple is abnormal. The reason being internalization and suppression have dominated his emotions with the result that he no longer experiences an emotional reaction when he sees others argue. In fact, conflict has become part of his ego that he frequently engages in dissensions without recognizing the negative impact on himself and others. There is a lack of self-control when the ego has normalized negative behaviors due to this prolonged suppression and internalization. Once he became aware of this, he was able to assess his situations, emotions, and reactions to signal himself toward regulation.

Trauma is an indefinite indicator of impact to the ego that is like a deep cut requiring longer healing time and intensive interventions. When one has been abused, the ego can go to an extreme inversion that shapes and conditions one's value system and self-projection. For example, a child that was physically abused by his parents cannot make sense of it or denies it, as they experience deep pain from this. The child only longs for his parent's love, yet abuse can alter the ego in many destructive ways. This boy grew up always forcing others to like him through aggression. When someone is unable to show him love, he rages and enforces it, leading his relationships to falter. He then turns to substance abuse to numb his emotional pain and confusion of why no one can love him. He finally engages in counseling to acquire a transpicuous assessment of his situation that begins the process of deconditioning. An assessment compels deep insight into whether a dilemma even exists. Therefore, awareness is the next step to comprehend the damages caused to the ego.

The second step is awareness, an awareness of how damaged one's ego is and understanding how it developed. When a child experiences a stressor, whether it was the parent's good intention or not, a subconscious thought births its own interpretation toward internal subjectivity. An example could be a little girl always seeking to please her father but finds him not attentive to her needs. Father rarely has time to ask about her day or compliment her. He does this because he was never praised, and he feels that keeping his distance from his daughter would be more beneficial to her than saying something wrong. He leaves her upbringing to the mother. Yet the girl only seeks her father's attention. The father has his own reasons for not being attentive to his daughter and is unable to communicate with her. The girl grows up thinking that she is unlikeable to her father and to other men, and as a result she does what it takes to please men. She finds herself sacrificing her time, money, body, energy to gain their attention. Once she became aware of how her negative thought processes developed, she was able to detach from the invalid thoughts that have been driving her negative behaviors. This awareness envisages connections from her past to the present. Many people repress the past or consider the past irrelevant, however the past helps bring light to our present state, augmenting our awareness of the issues. This is crucial in the process for change toward self-approbation.

The third step is acceptance. This is a formidable process to begin. To accept that one has been conditioned to their negative thoughts and accept how it developed is another key step in the process. Can you accept who you have become through your past? Are you ready to move forward? These are crucial questions to ask the self. Can one begin to accept who they have become through external conditioning factors? To accept that one's caregivers are held responsible for negative conditioning is unfathomable, especially if it was done without ill intentions. This becomes arduous for most people, as they associate placement of responsibility on caregivers analogous to disowning them. However, this is not the case when we separate our love for our caregivers from the resentment of their choices and behaviors. One can still love or like their caregivers yet hold them responsible for their choices. If that is too difficult, one can blame or hold responsible the caregiver's upbringing/environment or situations that forced them to make certain choices, since blaming them may be more difficult for the ego. Acceptance of ego damage and negative conditioning hopefully ignites tenacity for change through action.

The last step is action. Upon assessment, awareness, and acceptance of one's ego state, ego plasticity requires one to begin the process of reconditioning the ego and amending it to become more positive. This requires intentional, conscious effort applied to every thought, decision, and action. As much negativity ruminates through the mind, that much more one must captivate it and override it with positivity. Although the positive thought may not feel genuine or true, ruminating on it ameliorates the ego toward alacrity. The goal to reverse negative conditioning is to catch it, refute it, and cease it from being prolonged. Reducing intensity and frequency is the primary goal, not abatement. Action includes redirection, replacement, and proclamation. There is power in saying things out loud, which can override what is internal. Saying it to the self or others is healing to the ego. Then the ego begins to stretch and recondition itself toward positivity. This process is considered ego plasticity. The ego fluctuates and begins to change as one makes intentional choices to think, believe, and say positive self-affirmations.

Ego Partition

As one transforms through ego plasticity, the old self to the new, there are remnants of the past difficult to separate from. The ego can be attached with another person that continues to impact one's belief system, values, and thought processes. Conditioned beliefs or internal voices circulate within the ego system, making it difficult to identify the problem. The voices lead to guilt, sad feelings, discouragement, hopelessness, despair, blame, anger, and so on. These are negative emotions that should be identified, yet not prolonged. If these voices are frequent, the mood and behaviors will emulate negativity that is difficult to change. Therefore, the ego must segregate from the source that is causing these negative influences, which I call ego partition, a divide between parts of the ego that are not supporting it (Dictionary.com). This is extremely difficult for those who have been attached to a particular person for a long time. The past can be more powerful than the present or future.

Identifying the source of one's negative thoughts and feelings is crucial to begin segregation. Once identified, the associated negative thought is deflected away from one's ego. Dividing the external judgment and intrusive thoughts away from the ego yet maintaining the relationship is the goal. For example, a college student who grew up with a single mother begins to feel depressed. She is reminded of her mother's message that she can't be lazy and needs to do better with her grades and relationships. As she notices her grades falling and her relationships withering, she becomes more depressed, engaging in self-blame. She wakes up thinking about how her mother will judge her and be disappointed with her grades. She is afraid to go against her mother's demands and begins to have insomnia. To partition the negative thoughts would be to undermine her mother, causing her more anxiety. How could she disown her mother? How could she defy her demands when all her life she grew up in compliance with her directives? Her mother is all she has, and the thought of detaching from her exacerbates her anxiety and depression.

Ego partition in this situation would mean that she would internally deflect the voices in her head, while to her mother externally nodding her head, changing the subject, shortening the conversation, or making an excuse and walking away. This would reduce the distress of listening to mother's commands, deflecting negativity away from her ego, not allowing her mother's words to seep into her confidence and defining who she is. She would maintain her relationship with her mother yet set boundaries for herself based on her capacity to listen when she is saying discouraging things. She realized that her mother is unable to accept any assertive communication from her, therefore she shortens the conversation and changes it whenever she feels her mother is blaming her. She uses her inner voice to say things like, "My mother has high standards for me, and that is her issue, not mine, to meet," "I know I am doing my best, and I will set realistic expectations for myself." One can love the person yet dislike their actions and words. Setting boundaries can be in silence utilizing inner voice to affirm the ego and not allow the negative messages to ring true. Some need to express themselves on how it is affecting them, and for others it is more beneficial to keep it to themselves for the sake of the relationship. The ego may need separation from negative influences although they are from people they love. It is only the negative belief systems, thoughts, opinions, judgment, etc. that are being segregated rather than the person. We create multiple barriers from external factors to protect the ego from negative influences. The ego is protected by deflecting others' judgments away from it.

CHAPTER 6

Interventions

Aptitude Expansion

Aptitude is the "capability; ability; innate capacity for something" (Dictionary.com, n.d.) It is not something you can see or touch, yet it's a powerful agent of change. Each one of us has an aptitude to overcome challenges resulting in expansion that increases capacities to be prepared for further challenges. Accepting this world as a series of challenges is more realistic than hoping that our lives would continue without struggles. Many fear failure, yet failure reduces future failures. If one can accept their failure to be a teaching lesson to improve future opportunities, then only success can become the outcome. Most of our challenges arise from limited capacities resulting from fear of failure, immobilizing our ability to grow.

Capacities can come in many shapes and forms. Capacity is defined as "the ability to receive or contain," "the maximum amount that can be received or contained," "mental ability," as well as the power to perform or persevere (Dictionary.com, n.d.) We all carry capacities with a limit that cannot be surpassed, yet situations force it upon us. When our limit is reached, we either want to hide or run away, leading us toward depression or anxiety and impulsiveness without care for consequences. Limited capacities can be the source of the issue when it comes to change. We often look at others and find ourselves measuring our worth based on what we don't have or have not yet achieved. People are born with different capacities in various areas and can be stunted in expanding them due to various stressors or lack of support.

What types of capacities are there? Financial, emotional, intellectual, physical, spiritual, mental, and functional are just a few that come to mind. Working on expanding each of these can increase growth toward well-being and desired goals. The issues with expanding these capacities can be extremely difficult, as it requires accepting mistakes and learning from them to move forward. Letting go of barriers that stunt your growth, saying no to what is familiar and safe yet harmful. Rejecting negative thoughts that turn you away from expansion. Many times, stressors and conditions of living that are out of one's control suppress this growth and ability to expand. However, finding things that are within your control, such as changing perspective and deflecting negative thoughts, can expand your capacity in small amounts. Many people want large amounts of change, but the small, slow persistence change can be more powerful and lasting. Troubles hit and it seems "if only the circumstances could be lifted everything would be better," "if only that person could change or go away," "if only I was born into a better family." The thoughts persist and overshadow any capacity left to sustain one through these difficult challenges. The darkness seems to cover the light, yet light can be found in darkness if one chooses to see what is not visible.

A teenager is stuck at home taking care of siblings while a single mother is always working. The teenager sacrifices her interests and future to manage the present situation due to her mother's incapacities. The teenager feels guilty when she wants to pursue her own interests and is unable to find support to get her the means and experience to pursue it. Her mother constantly says that they will not have any home to live in or food to eat if she doesn't help out with household tasks and taking care of siblings. Both the mother and teenager have limited capacities in their situation that makes them feel they are circling in the same direction without any change or progress. How can they maximize their situation and move toward expanding their aptitude? The teenager's best hope is to do well in her education given the time she has to herself to ensure some possibilities. The teenager can create her own support network to help her through any barriers or challenges. The teenager can also create a detailed schedule to complete the necessities for survival and carve out time for what is critical to her own success. Moving forward with understanding and accepting her situation may be the start, then ruminating on positive thoughts, such as, "This is temporary. I will get out of this, and there will be a day I can help my family." Utilizing her down time with things that could expand her aptitude, improving her future. Most of the time is wasted when ruminating on "what ifs" and "why me?" Wishfully thinking that this situation could be different could deter us from our goals. Every situation varies, so there is not a right answer or one way to resolve it. Therefore, many options and solutions exist if one can surpass the negative rumination about their situation.

A couple finds themselves in a dull relationship that makes one cheat on the other. When the wife finds out, there is mistrust, hatred, and hopelessness. The wife can't get past the reality of this situation and resents her husband for cheating on her. The children make it difficult for the wife to end the relationship. The wife is constantly reminded of infidelity, and the relationship is forever changed. The husband does his best to sustain their relationship and make it work, however everything is a trigger for her. How does the wife expand her aptitude? The wife may need some time for herself and healing. She seeks her own therapy and processes her distress. The wife explores her options and makes a decision based on having slightly more pros than cons. Her children are her priority, and therefore she chooses to keep it a functional relationship for now. She finds other ways to feel secure in this unstable relationship. The wife enrolls in classes that are of her interest and starts living her life. She is at peace that if the relationship ever ends, she has optimized her opportunities to pursue her future and interests. Can the relationship ever go back to the way it was? Probably not. However, the wife did not choose to stay sullen and sulking in despair, instead placing all her energy on creating opportunities for her success and children's happiness. She knew that if it happened again that would be the end of their relationship. She shifted her focus away from the "what ifs," moving on to to "if he does, he is out." The shift in perspective can make all the difference in overcoming despair. The wife also understood that it would take a lot of time to heal from such a betrayal. The passage of time was necessary for things to improve.

These are just a few of the examples that have shown how even despairing situations can have aptitude expansion. Many times, we stay stuck in our situation as we hope for it to change or desire to change the past. Although one knows this doesn't happen, it feels safer to hope for it. What are some ways to expand your aptitude? The first step is understanding the situation and accepting it for what it is. The next step is to explore solutions that are more immediate. Then creating a network of support is key to overcoming as we all need people around us to validate us and recognize our efforts. Spiritual support can go above our limited human capacity. Sometimes human limitations call for spiritual expansion to arise beyond the situation. There are many situations where no one can help, impossible for change, and uncontrollable circumstances.

These are moments when the ego cannot sustain itself, therefore accessing one's spirituality can create internal security.

Emotional Constipation

Culture has defined our state of emotion to be emotionless. Crying is viewed as a weakness, creating isolation. Anger ignites guilt, is treated as evil, and causes division. Happiness can be a facade for others or cause jealousy. Sadness brings separation as well as denial. Our culture and society have its own judgment about how we should express our emotions or suppress them. Our emotions can be deceiving or impossible to manage. The emotion circulates to intensify then deflates. Its uncontrollable role eliminates rational thinking. How can something be so influential?

Emotional security is an innate longing that can be disregarded if other basic needs are not met. Most of the time our physical needs, such as food and shelter, are primal. Once those are met, our need for emotional security surfaces in our consciousness. How do we define emotional security? I believe another word for emotional security is secure attachment. Is this attainable when it has been voided most of one's life? An individual who lacks emotional security may not be conscious of it, especially when there is an inadequate supply of other basic needs such as food, shelter, or financial limitations. The capacity to deepen relationships is insufficient when basic needs are unmet.

Emotion when experienced can bring to life excitement and thrills while on the other hand sorrow and pain. The important thing to remember is that it can be elongated or temporary. The existence of emotions is not a bad thing; it is the prolonged intensity of emotion that can cause damage. Our emotions are influenced by our thoughts and perspectives. It can be altered depending on what thought processes you choose to guide you. Grief from a significant loss is a natural emotion that signifies the depth of love for that person and is not an emotion that needs to be ceased quickly or instantly. There is a healing process that is necessary with support. Our negative emotions can lead to increased depression or anxiety. This is when emotions can cause more damage. Working toward emotional expression and expansion of aptitude is key to discharging emotional constipation.

Many times, the negative emotion from a situation is suppressed, causing a volcano effect of buildup waiting to explode or inhibited to cause medical or mental health issues. I call this emotional constipation. Just like our digestive system, constipation can cause issues to our internal organs, eventually affecting other parts of our body if not processed outward. Our emotions work the same way. The negative emotions need to be processed outward or they compile and affect other parts of our wellbeing. Compilation of these emotions can become destructive to the self. Thoughts and belief systems can be altered due to this. Therefore, the negative emotions for all situations recalled past and present need to be processed to rectify a healthier ego system. Many of us may stay stuck in emotional constipation, stalling any insight or progress. Although it may not matter for some, for others it can destroy relationships and self-achievements. What are some ways to process these emotions? A safe and confidential way is with a professional therapist who one feels comfortable and safe to share with. I recommend finding a therapist through a referral or trial and error to see which one is a good fit, as it will vary for many people. Other ways of expression can be through mindfulness practices, music, physical exercise, aroma therapy, self-care activities, speaking to a friend or family member, prayer, or even positive self-talk utilizing an inner voice.

A female adult realizes that she has harbored anger toward her mother for not protecting her from other family members. She was physically abused by other family members when her mother was out working, although she knew about it and didn't do anything. For the longest time, she was confused how a mother could ignore the situation and not believe many of the things she was telling her. The female adult began to suppress her feelings of anger, while justifying her mother's need for work to provide food on the table. She began to believe that maybe she deserved the abuse. She then begins to see how her depression and lack of social interactions are impacting her functioning at work and socially. She has a hard time acknowledging her feelings of anger and processing them due to fear of disowning her mother.

It wasn't until therapy that she realized her false beliefs were driving her fears. Whenever she is reminded of the physical abuse, she would ignore the memories and stop herself from being angry at her mother. She went as far to blame herself for the abuse, as that seemed easier. However, little did she know this led to self-neglect and destruction. She was used to suppressing her anger toward mother due to her guilt. The compilation of anger turned into depression and lack of motivation for her life. She became emotionally constipated, causing damage to her mental health. It wasn't until she found the courage to share her true feelings to her therapist and began to unravel her feelings toward her mother. At first it was easier to express her anger toward her perpetrators. Then slowly she began to realize she had more anger toward her mother hidden in her subconscious. It had never surfaced until therapy.

As the therapist normalized her feelings, she was led to discard negative thoughts that led to blame, guilt, and shame. There were misconceptions preventing expression of emotions. Once she was able to speak about her past and share how she really felt, a release of freedom ignited, as if she no longer was imprisoned by her fears to express her emotions. She realized that she could still love her mother for who she is and the good things she did accomplish yet be angry at her choices and lack of protection and support. Once she was able to separate the two, she didn't have an issue with expressing her negative feelings related to her mother. This is an example of how the outward expression of our negative emotions is so crucial to our wellbeing. Emotional constipation can impact multiple areas of our lives. It is a matter of when one will begin emotional discharge to prevent further damage to the self. There are steps to assist this process.

Finding Leverage

Another method to enhance self-approbation is to find your leverage. Everyone has something they can contribute to others or oneself. Many relationships exist due to having leverage, whether it be sharing the same blood in a family, support, emotional attachment, financial gain, power, fame, mutuality, similarity, companionship, sharing children, working toward a common goal, working partner, productivity, compatibility, similar interests, generosity, materialism, pleasurable activities, and so on. Everyone has something to offer, but many times it is difficult for one to see what leverage they have, especially if one feels indebted to that person or is clouded by self-neglect and self-hatred. It is important for one to identify their areas of strength and reasons others need them.

A wife is constantly walking on eggshells to avoid aggravating her husband, yet he is more frustrated or angered by her actions. The wife is constantly blamed for things and feels responsible for their arguments. Many times, the husband twists the words to make the wife feel she is responsible for everything and is at his mercy. The wife cannot find any leverage over her husband, who seems to take advantage of her and easily bosses her around. Through therapy, the wife discovers that her income and ability to take care of household tasks means leverage over her husband. She starts asserting her needs to carry on a conversation when the husband is calm. She negotiates doing certain tasks once the husband can fulfill his responsibility. The wife leaves dishes and insists for them to be done for her to cook dinner. The husband is used to the wife cooking and cleaning after, but the wife realizes that he is taking advantage of this and expects this to be done by her. The wife requests that the husband help around more based on what he is willing to do. At first there is a battle between them, but the husband slowly begins to see he needs her as she persistently balances their responsibilities. She notices that he is starting to respect her and no longer takes things for granted. She has found value in herself and realized that she has something to give in the relationship and took a risk of losing her husband in the process of change by asserting her leverage.

There may be a risk when shifting toward self-approbation, therefore each person needs to make that determination. One must ask, "Is it worth trying for better results or remain with my life as is?" Whatever the decision, there are pros and cons to all of them. Neither one may be easy or yield the desired results, but a path not discovered or never walked may never help you find out if there was anything better. In the example above, the wife could have continued to live at her husband's mercy due to her fears of losing him or her family. The consequence of this was feeling unhappy, burning out, depression and persistent self-neglect. Through therapy she was able to heal and work toward taking care of her needs and finding a positive way to address it to her husband.

Another example is a guy who is fearful of losing his girlfriend and is at her mercy. He buys her things, does everything she tells him to do, and supports her in every way possible. He notices that she doesn't respect him and is fearful that she will leave him. He has difficulty finding leverage over her and displays low self-esteem. He believes that no one will be with him except her. This creates a one-way relationship, but he feels secure staying in this relationship despite his needs being neglected. His fear of being abandoned is greater than taking care of his needs. What leverage can he find in himself? He soon realizes that he is the only one who would tolerate her personality as others distance themselves from her. He reduces his efforts when it is at a disadvantage to him and sets boundaries when it is inconvenient for him. He realizes that his willingness to adjust and put up with her personality is leverage and uses that to balance the relationship. The girlfriend starts to respect him and longs for his attentiveness. She starts doing things for him, and they find mutuality with each other. Once he found his leverage, the relationship became more balanced, and they were able to respect each other's needs and compromise based on each of their interests. In some situations, the partner may oppose these changes and choose to leave the relationship or have a severe reaction that can make things strenuous. It may be difficult to predict how the other person will respond. However, if one can find their leverage, whether the partner leaves or not, they have found themselves and their value that deserves to be respected. Eventually, they will be surrounded by people who respect them for who they are and choose to be. Although the fear of losing someone was greater, the experience of being respected was worth it. This change was possible with the support of loving friends, family, and his therapist.

CHAPTER 7

Finding Sustainable Happiness

Sustainable happiness, is it possible? Many would spend thousands of dollars and colossal amounts of time and energy to attain sustainable happiness. I have yet to meet anyone who has experienced happiness for long periods of time. There are many who have temporary happiness or pleasure even on a frequent basis. However, it always seems to have an end or limited duration as negative situations dissolve any remaining happiness. Happiness is usually sought after through conditional things, hoping it will sustain itself permanently. When it is not sustainable, one goes through any measure to attain it. Conditional items, such as people and materials are unpredictable and uncontrollable that make it difficult to guarantee sustained happiness.

I conducted an anonymous survey through Survey Monkey that was posted on social media sites, such as Facebook as well as through Survey Monkey to obtain respondents. The number of respondents was from 299-561 participants. This survey was to see how often people feel happiness, the duration of happiness, and the contributing factors.

The questions and results were the following:

1. Are you a minority? 52.96% not a minority, 47.14% minority.

2. What is your socioeconomic status? The highest was average income at 64.94%, below average at 20.21%, and above average at 14.85%.

3. What is your gender? Female responses were highest at 60.64%, male at 37.57% and less than 1% were others.

4. What is your age range? The top age range of participants were ages 45-54 at 26.25%, 25-34 at 19.29%, 35-44 at 17.14%, 55-64 at 13.39%, 18-24 at 10.54%, 65+ at 9.46%, and under 3% were ages 5-17.

5. How often do you feel happiness (Feelings of joy, pleasure, or satisfaction)? Answers included: Almost daily, several times a week, several times a month, several times a year, rarely/never. The top answer was almost daily at 44.92%, several times a week at 34.40%, several times a month at 15.51%, several times a year at 6.77%, and rarely/never at 4.28%.

6. Which contributing factor has made you feel most happy? There was a drop-down list of various items to choose from or to list your own. The top four most contributing factors to happiness were family at 39.96%, partner at 12.41%, relationships (e.g., friends, socialization) at 13.14%, and faith/religion at 13.14%.

7. How long does your happiness last each occurrence? The top was several hours at 38.13%, several minutes at 24.41%, a full day at 17.73%, several days at 7.69%, constantly without ceasing at 6.69%, none of the above at 2.01%, weeks at 1.67%, months at 1.34%, and a year at 0.33%.

This survey concluded that happiness is short lived yet can be as frequent as daily when it comes to family or relationships. This shows how relationships are a major contributing factor for sustainable happiness. This may explain how relationships at an early age can have so much impact on one's mental health and ego formation. We are social by nature, yet relationships are one of the most challenging things to control or repair. Sustainable happiness may not be realistic for some, however extending the duration and frequency of happiness is within reach. The self must take control towards unconditional acceptance for sustainable happiness to exist. The big question: How can this be done?

Balanced Life

Many people look for answers, a textbook script on success, a detailed list of what to do, however life does not work out the same for everyone. Although situations may be similar, each of us is unique, and we need to find value in this. Therefore, any specific step-by-step script for success may be temporary or unsuccessful unless one discovers their own script, created by the self. We take in information, examples, autobiographies, advice, readings, etc., yet we filter what applies to ourselves in the present situation and leave out what may not apply at this time or may not be advantageous. We explore outcomes by making decisions and choices based on present information and situation. We learn by the outcomes and advance in search of improvement each time. Many times, people fear making mistakes or making the wrong decision, however only experience can confirm if it was a mistake or a benefit. The key term is "balance."

Balance is difficult to find. It can be mastered when you start making decisions and learn from them. Sometimes you can go from one extreme to the other to figure out where the balance is. It is our fears of imperfections that prevent us from finding this balance. All decisions come with pros and cons. A successful person knows how to move on from a failed decision and utilize it as a learning experience. We need balance in our parenting, relationships, habits, activities, and so forth. People are quick to judge others or themselves rather than accepting their place and moving forward from that situation. Others' judgments create barriers to our success as we place much value on what they think or say. Most of the time people are not judging us based on our assumptions, rather our negative ego or negative thought processes keep feeding into those messages. Balanced living is different for everyone.

Many of us come from different cultures, environments, history, trauma, family, spirituality, and so forth that it is nearly impossible to have the same solution for everyone. "How can I find my balance?" We start with where you are today with your thought processes, life circumstances, belief systems, values, and spirituality. Many of the issues arise from dissatisfaction with our current situation and fears of not achieving anything in the future. When we disdain the present, we are incognizant of the possibility for change, finding ourselves twirling in circles back at the same place. The past weighs us down, and the future creates uncertainty and anxiety. Therefore, the present is the only thing we have complete control of that can become the agent of change. The process starts with creating filters and discerning which beliefs and thoughts need to be weeded out that are negatively impacting our present lives. It is like a chemical facial peel, where layers of outer skin cells are taken off for new healthier skin to grow back. If you don't remove the dead skin cells, there is no room for the new skin to grow. This is like our ego system that is covered with layers of hurt, pain, trauma, insecurities, desire to be accepted and loved, faulty beliefs, and much more. If these layers are not recognized and processed in a healthy manner, it can be difficult to make positive changes. To stay stagnant in a familiar place is found easier than change. What was so familiar is enticing to continue, yet harmful to the ego. Familiarity is more powerful than change. It provides consistency, security, predictability, and comfort that humanism is more subject to live by. We tend to lean toward familiarity hoping that it would provide a better life. In some instances, this can be true while in others there are more detrimental consequences than desired. Those that desire change need to feel free to make mistakes, learn from them, and grow toward a balanced life.

Just like the removal of a chemical facial peel, the redness and visible presentation ignites worry and concern. However, for a healthy process it takes time and experience to learn what fits best with one's skin before glowing skin can resurface. Once the old filters are removed, one can feel bare and uncertain on how to think, behave, and act. One can start by identifying desired and potential characteristics to attain. Then practice exhibiting these characteristics and making choices that attend to the ego rather than neglecting it or being pretentious. In the beginning discomfort overwhelms as one goes against their own nature. At this stage support is needed due to the weight of negativity, both cognitively and emotionally. It is recommended to seek out a professional mental health provider or evaluate progress through a self-esteem measure, such as the Self-Compassion scale (Neff, 2016).

The next phase is finding balance as you practice new characteristics. Balance can be found by merely implementing what is needed to feed your ego with love and support. The fears of implementing this can be overcome by practicing and experiencing the benefits or learning from the mistakes. Like any other new skill being learned, trial and error needs to occur to determine which ones are effective to implement for next time. Making mistakes and failing is part of the process, like learning any new skill or sport. This is required to improve the skill and learn how to master it. We all learn to drive with the brakes on the left side and accelerator on the right. If I was to switch the brakes and accelerator pads in a car or the handlebars of a bicycle to learn a different way of driving or riding, one would need to practice multiple times to master it, and multiple accidents are inevitable. Those who drive or ride bikes know that the functions come naturally to our bodies, where we do not have to think about how to turn with our hands or drive with our feet, as they are conditioned to do what was learned and practiced from the beginning. Repetition can reduce the level of effort required. Deconditioning the mind is just as difficult and requires frequent practice and time to be familiar with a new way of thinking.

Balanced Parenting

Many parents feel inadequate or engage in self-blame for not raising their children to certain expectations. There are so many parenting techniques and tools, however is there only one way to parent a "perfect" child? If a parent follows a step-by-step tool in parenting their children, would that significantly change them? Parents have their own ego states that consist of their own insecurities, upbringing, culture, expectations, and subjective opinion about what is best for their child. Therefore, how can parenting be a textbook with specific steps to attain their desired outcome? In my opinion, every parent must find their own balance based on their ego states and who they are. Of course, a parent can improve their ego state and have better outcomes. I highly recommend a life coach or therapist to support a parent to find their right balance.

What do I mean by balance? A mother who was physically abused by her father continues to shy away from any type of discipline toward her own children due to fear she will become like her father. She feels judged by other parents and teachers about her lack of discipline toward her children. As her children get out of control, she feels incompetent as a parent. Her guilt overrides her ability to set boundaries and ensure her children follow rules. Her fears of being hated by her children, as she detested her father, paralyzed her to speak to her children. How can this mother improve her parenting as her children continue to misbehave? First, this mother would benefit from her own individual therapy to process her own past trauma and overcome her feelings of guilt. This is her step toward finding a balance. As she is working on this, she begins to implement small steps toward disciplining her children. She may not be able to be consistent on her directives or consequences, however with others' support she was able to start creating a parenting style based on her abilities, capacities, and fears. As she compares herself with other mothers, she envies their strength, which affirms her efforts in replicating their strategies based on her comfort level.

It is important for a parent to understand their own limitations and capacities. Without this, they are unable to create realistic expectations for themselves. Most parents live with unrealistic expectations that hinder them from moving toward becoming a balanced parent. In balanced parenting, a parent is not judged by their outcome. Yet they are accountable for what they are doing to gain support in working toward becoming a better parent. The specific tools and methods are there to give parents options to select from, not to feel judged for lack of implementation. Once a parent feels incompetent, it goes down a spiral of negativity that prevents them from moving forward and learning from their parenting mistakes. Giving grace to the self for the past and normalizing mistakes are key components to becoming a balanced parent.

Therefore, "balance" can be defined as the place where one feels competent to learn from their mistakes. Accepting their efforts given their limitations. Identifying one's weakness, limitations, capacities, strengths, abilities, willingness, and resources are key to balanced parenting. Many times, it is due to lack of insight in these areas that keep parents stunted in repeated patterns of negative outcomes that are unsatisfactory. Consider the variance in culture, ideology, values, morals, beliefs, upbringing, circumstances, resources, perspective, and so on that need to be considered for every parent. Most of us maintain generalizations about what a good parent is and easily judge each other. I have yet to meet a parent that is 100% satisfied with the turnout of their children. Are most parents seeking something that doesn't exist? I believe so. It is our unrealistic expectations that set us up for failure and disappointment repeatedly.

A mother speaks about her son, who she wishes was more aggressive and less sensitive, while another mother speaks about her son who is always getting into trouble, conflict with peers, and is too competitive. The son who is more sensitive has advantages of being favored by teachers and other peers as he gets along well with them, but he lacks aggression in sports and is unable to excel in most activities. He was raised with attentiveness from parents and validation of negative emotions as he expects the same from those around him. His feelings are easily hurt. The other son has no fear of death or fighting peers, was popular in school, and always succeeded in any sports. He had a drive to be the best, and it didn't matter whose feelings were hurt as he rarely showed any emotions. Parenting can have advantages and disadvantages to our children, and whichever has been conducted the results both have pros and cons. Therefore, comparison is not valid. The question should not be, "Why is my child like this?" It should be, "How can I help my child succeed based on their present attributes?" As parents, we need to reduce self-blame and no longer strive for something that does not exist, yet work with what is in the present.

Balanced parenting allows a parent to start from where they are as parents and expand areas of weakness, limitations, and hesitancy. No parent is allowed to judge another as the focus is on the self and where the self can improve. What steps can I take today? What support do I have? How can I know about my limitations and capacities with parenting? Which resources can I acquire? These are self-reflection questions to consider as one moves toward self-awareness, the key to balanced parenting. One can find their balance as they test various methods of parenting and learn from their mistakes. A parent does not need to worry about failing as each situation will bring balance by reflecting on the pros and cons, improving each time until the desired outcome is established. Changing strategies that no longer work and learning alternative methods from others or the community for support. Our measure of achievement foremost is asking oneself, "Did I do my best in executing good parenting skills?" "Best" includes self-awareness and utilizing one's resources. A small effort to get started on this positive pathway is all that is needed. Secondly, are the outcomes different? This can indicate whether something has changed. Although every situation varies, most of the time there is a slight change in how the parent feels or thinks and/or how the child behaves. As the child gets older, parents' control, directives, expectations, and boundaries shift. For children heading into their teens, family team meetings with mutual decision making or understanding of the consequences of actions are necessary. Teen involvement in establishing rules or making decisions should become mutual unless safety is a concern or trust has been broken.

Many parents prioritize outcomes, results, behaviors, rules, morals, culture over relationships. For a child, relationships are at the forefront along with obtaining what they want. This causes a relational discrepancy that dismantles any progress for healthy engagement. The key is to bridge the discrepancy and reunite the broken pieces. For example, a parent is unable to get their child to comply with their directives. They implement many consequences, reward systems, and efforts to communicate the order. However, the child is persistently noncompliant and asserting her interests only increases angry outbursts. The parent is uncertain about ways to address the child. Finally, through therapy the therapist builds a relationship with the child and models the parent on ways to engage the child in a connecting manner. As the parent focuses on enhancing the relationship, the child begins to soften as they express each other's thoughts and feelings. The child yearned for a positive engagement and was defiant to anything when there was no relationship in place. Once a relationship was established, the parent was able to maintain the rules and values, creating a structured environment with some flexibility to the child's needs. The parent was more attuned to the child's cues, such as hunger, fatigue, stress at school, stressors at home, etc. There was more flexibility with rules and procedures to emphasize the importance of the relationship to the child. Relationship, structure, and consistency are healthy components to establish when becoming a balanced parent.

Relationships

We are social by nature, yearning for connections. Yet it seems relationships can be hurtful, harmful, unappreciated, and lack reciprocity. Many people yearn for deep relationships in social circles with unrealistic expectations. People attend events in hopes of finding someone to connect with or to enjoy each other's company. Whatever the reason, we all crave relational connection, though some are isolated due to fears of human connection. Why is it that things desirable can be so harmful? The varied ego states attempting to connect create a ruckus rather than harmony. "If only that person could be this way with me" is the hopeful expectation in relationships. There are layers of relationships, and outer layers are those that we surround ourselves with due to work as acquaintances. Sometimes this includes family members that require distance. The next layer are those relationships you are interested in meeting outside of work or in the usual environment. They can be your hangout buddies or companions who share similar interests. The core circle is who you feel safe and trust enough to let your guard down, maintaining an emotional attachment. The inner core circle usually consists of only a few people if not only one. If we do not divide our social circle into these sections, then one expects everyone to be part of the core or accepted by all. This is where disappointment can happen. Learning to accept that people may not have the capacity or willingness to connect at a deeper level is helpful for the ego. It can deter self-blame and self-neglect. It is common to feel inadequate when people are not responding or engaging in a manner to reflect their interest in you. A healthy ego would say to oneself, "That is their loss," and move on. As one shifts toward a self-approbated ego, relationships change as healthier people get drawn to this ego.

An adult male grew up wanting to please others to feel valued. He would be at the mercy of his coworkers and peers to ensure that he is doing everything right for them to like him. He was unaware of self-negligence, as he was convinced that doing things for others would gain their approval. As years went by, the demands increased, while his mood became more depressed. He felt worse each day yet continued to make efforts to gain their approval. As soon as he realized that these people did not have the right to place value on his worth, he was no longer at their mercy nor trying so hard to accommodate them. He began to reach out to his peers with similar interests to engage in an activity together. He realized that these people were not meant to be part of his inner core circle, however great to engage in activities for social purposes. The inner core circle was just a few who had been there with him the longest, accepting him without any pretense.

Couples

Partner relationships have become challenging as both pursue love, acceptance, and understanding from one another. A vast disconnect exists as each person focuses on obtaining their needs from the other partner. Is it realistic to expect your partner to love unconditionally? This is a longing people have when entering relationships, especially in long-term commitments, such as marriage. Can attraction and mutual interests be enough to sustain a couple's relationship? There are various reasons people enter into partner relationships. Some enter relationships out of chemistry and feelings, yet they seem to dissolve so quickly. Some end up in a functional relationship or self-sacrificial due to limited financial means, fears of leaving, or for children's wellbeing. One cannot judge the other for their choices. Partner reconciliation becomes strenuous when each person places the emphasis on the other person to change. If this was controllable, a solution would exist. If you find yourself in the same situation, then your methodology is ineffective. Understanding your partner and finding ways to work around their innate habits and personalities is more effective. Although relationships can be situational, one would need to evaluate if those are unable to be changed. If that is the case, then one needs to weigh the pros and cons of that relationship to choose what is more beneficial. Safety is the utmost important factor in a relationship. If safety is at risk, it becomes a dangerous situation that no one should have to endure. Finding resources and support may be necessary.

In couples therapy, I work on any critical issues then move toward building each ego toward self-approbation. As each person works on their own ego, this transformation makes it easier to bridge the gaps in the relationship and execute effective solutions. Each couples' process differs and carries historical experiences that may need to be processed. Most of the couples I have treated had underlying issues from their past that were affecting their present relationship. Their negative ego states were disabling any progress to work together on their issues. In the beginning, any conversations that led to intense arguments were not encouraged until the skills were developed, and self-awareness was present. For Christian couples, the institute of marriage was created by God. Therefore, God-centered lives are necessary for the relationship to thrive or sustain itself. As each person focuses on their spirituality to improve their ego states, the union will thrive. Overall, the shift in focus apart from the partner and on to the self is key in couples' relationships, since the self is what one can control 100%. Most of the time it is the innate characteristics of one's partner that are irritating and intolerable. Therefore, they spend all their energy trying to change this, yet it worsens or never changes. If the partner is doing what they can with their innate nature to be managed 50% of the time, that is the most one can expect. This is usually reached after couples or individual therapy.

A couple comes to therapy due to dissatisfaction in their marriage, yet both want to maintain it due to the children. The couple have lost interest in each other and are constantly bickering. They realized that ever since having children the overwhelming tasks have burned them out, and their relationship has been unstable ever since. Each person expects the other to do more and feels tasks are unevenly shared. They argue about finance, have not had any physical intimacy, and lost interest in mutual activities. The couple began to redefine their present goals and let go of their hopes for marriage to be as they first met. The wife wanted her husband to treat her as he did when they first met. The husband felt his wife no longer respected him as she once did. As they focused on the past, they were unable to move forward. Once they understood that their situation is different and other things now attract them, they were able to set reasonable goals and alternate activities of interest together. Their goal of staying together for the children was of the utmost importance for them.

As they witnessed their partner process their own upbringing and self-neglected ego, empathy increased for one another. They accepted that for now their relationship is functional with a purpose to provide a supportive environment for their children to thrive. As they worked together on this goal, they began to enjoy each other's company again. They shifted their focus on what they could control and agreed to sacrifice/compromise something for their partner. It became a mutual/reciprocal relationship, where both benefited from each other's sacrifices. Working together on a mutual goal saved their marriage. Accepting intention over the negative behaviors enhanced their level of understanding for one another. Their realistic expectations of each other reduced their engagement in bottomless arguments. Expanding their capacities in areas of trust and understanding were also key components to their success. The therapist supported each of them to develop self-approbated egos to benefit the relationship.

Self-Approbated Ego

The goal is to attain a self-approbated ego. Due to layers of imposition to one's ego, it can be difficult to recognize what is the genuine self. Below are some simple steps to begin this process.

Step 1: Recognition—One must identify which thoughts, belief systems, decisions, emotions are being experienced in the moment. This identification helps to redirect or deflect them if not beneficial. One can get stuck at this stage, being unsure about their thoughts and emotions.

Step 2: Filtration—Once identified, there needs to be a filtering system for a healthy process. If we don't filter the negative thoughts and emotions and place them in the right place, it can cloud our judgment and make us act in ways that don't benefit our ego. We filter by acknowledging every possible thought and emotion as being helpful or not and deflect those that are not.

Step 3: Cessation—The positive thoughts and emotions can naturally dissolve into the ego system, but the negative ones need to be blocked promptly. Although the negative thoughts may feel true if they don't contribute to the ego, it can do more damage to the self. Therefore, ceasing negative thoughts in turn for feeding positivity to the ego will build the ego to its utmost esteemed position.

Step 4: Redirection—Once the negative thoughts cease, redirection is needed to overcome them. Otherwise, the negative thoughts continue to seep into the brain and try to make an impact repeatedly. Those who have a hard time refuting these thoughts remain stuck in a circling direction with no progress. Redirection can be through replacement with helpful thoughts or engaging in an activity that can reduce or cease negative thoughts. Therapy, external supports, and spiritual disciplines can assist with redirection when self is unable to do so.

Step 5: Self-Approbation—This is the most difficult stage and persistence is required. The conscious mind speaks to the subconscious to shift the perspective to benefit the ego. The inner voice reminds the ego that one is worthy and deserving of goodness. Many of the distress comes from the internal thoughts that are disguised with normalcy. One's thought process becomes a normal part of their daily functioning, so it is difficult to identify it as an issue. As one identifies, filters, ceases, and redirects negativity, self-approbation can grow and expand to further enhance the ego system. Maintaining self-approbation requires consistent internal self-talk toward self-affirmations along with inclusion activities, such as prayer, music, constructive post-it reminders, Ted talks, inspirational videos, meditations, supportive friends, and so on to remind the self how unconditionally loved they are.

Each person has varying levels of capacity for things that require expansion for improvement. Negative situations can expand these capacities to further stretch the ability to overcome past stressors. We all have certain limitations that can be expanded to enhance the ego and overcome stressors. Unfortunately, most of these are expanded through difficult challenges or taking risks in uncomfortable situations. Some of the beneficial areas to expand are levels of understanding, tolerance, control, responsibility, resiliency, trust/faith, and hopefulness. One of the most important expansions when dealing with people and situations that I have found is expanding the level of understanding for others and one's situation.

This prevents the buildup of anger and self-neglect, yet there is caution with ignoring the issues or suppressing them, which can be unhealthy. Therefore, a healthy balance of asserting one's needs yet expanding understanding of others is necessary. I believe self-assessment tools would be helpful to guide each person where they stand in each area. We all have some capacity in these areas, although some are higher or lower than others. There are limited self-assessment tests to signify these levels. Self-assessment tools can designate a starting point for self-improvement to further increase self-awareness. Self-awareness begins the process of change, however due to limited resources, I recommend future research in this area.

CHAPTER 8

Conclusion

Many of our issues appear to be presented at a conscious level, visibly noticeable by self and others. People strive to rectify their problems outwardly without addressing the source of the issue, which is underlying at the subconscious level. My work involves addressing the source of the issues that involve processing the layers of imposition from external factors that have fabricated the present self. This is the work of the ego system that is expandable to reshape and reconstruct toward a more genuine self. Not all people need ego transformation, nor is it possible for some. People are created to function despite their impositions and find a self they are satisfied with that doesn't require change. The need for change should be first identified by the self. When it is enforced by others, change is difficult to accomplish.

Is sustainable happiness possible? I believe it can be when the ego is reproduced by an unconditionally loving self and/or God. Happiness needs to come from within, controlled by the self. The self is the only one that can have the most consistent and sustainable management. Yet many allow others and external factors to control the self that leads them into despair or temporal happiness. If the self is unable to be managed in a healthy way, then the process of self-discovery toward inner healing is necessary. Our initial being was unconditionally loved with no conditions required to be valued or worthy. The worldly system we live in is centered on conditions for approval and worth. We cannot avoid the reality of our world nor drastically change the system. However, we can change the only thing that we have control over, which is the self. We can choose not to allow the conditions of this world to define our worth and value. Yet one can choose to engage in the conditions of this world for temporary pleasure without affecting one's value or worth. The conditions are everywhere around us, and therefore beginning the process of finding unconditional love for self is the start of changing conditions around you.

Many people strive to change their conditions first, yet when it doesn't work the disappointment is massive. I recommend reconstructing the ego to self-approbate and then see what conditions fall into place. I have witnessed naturally healthier relationships, an increase in confidence, changes in jobs, and a happier life. Many are still waiting for the worldly system that is corroding the ego to change. One must take hold of what one can change, which is the self to be the only judge. Since we were initially unconditionally loved beings, that spirit continues to live within us to unearth this through the self and/or God. As we find balance in our lives and leverage over situations, we can shift our perspectives to benefit the ego toward a healthier self.

An adult single mother raising three children on her own is overwhelmed, fatigued, insomnia, depressed, and anxious about her living situation. She sees no hope for her and her children's future. She feels guilty asking others for any help. She barely makes it to work, picks up the kids, and helps them with their homework. Her routine has discouraged her from any hope for the future for change. This mother has low self-esteem and a self-neglected ego that has tried to please others by doing what is right as a single mom caring for her children. Her capacity has been maximized, with no room left for any self-care or meeting her own needs. Her tolerance to stress is low, and she doesn't trust anyone. She feels she has no control of her situation, while blaming herself for their low standard of living. She begins to reach out to a therapist who begins the process of working through her guilt, reorganizing her day to reduce stress.

As she learns to let go of some responsibility, she finds herself with some energy for personal quiet time at night for a few minutes to breathe from the long day. She also began taking prayer walks outside to exercise and let God know that she is unable to do this on her own, asking for His peace. With the support of her therapist and faith, she was able to expand her capacity for control and responsibility. Most of her guilt was weighing her down, impairing her ability to parent with positivity. She expanded her understanding of her situation to be temporary and focused on enjoying her relationship with children. She worked through her guilt and self-blame along with obtaining support for additional financial aid through various programs introduced by other neighbors. Although her situation didn't change, her perspective and capacity of understanding, control, faith, and responsibility increased enough to help her get through each day. Accessing other support played a major role, since she knew she was unable to overcome her situation on her own.

The underlying dilemma to our issues in this world is the gap between the unconditional self, living in this conditional world judged by its own system. We need to move away from this conditional system through internal self-approbation. Does this mean we no longer seek conditional things? Not necessarily. Once the ego is self-approbated, seeking after conditions is recommended to enhance the ego, as it will no longer define its worth. The issues arise when the ego finds its worth in conditional things that increase depression and anxiety. The key to adapting to this world is reconstructing the ego to self-approbate and accessing additional support. This balance is not easy to attain, yet any effort is highly recommended. For those who have difficulty with self-approbation, finding a therapist or engaging one's spirit can open pathways to experiencing unconditional love through ego plasticity.

References

Bluth, K., Campo, R. A., Futch, W. S., & Gaylord, S. A. (2017). Age and gender differences in the associations of self-compassion and emotional well-being in A large adolescent sample. Journal of Youth and Adolescence, (4), 840. doi:10.1007/s10964-016-0567-2

Cha, S. H. S. (2021). *The Relationship between the Level of Self-Compassion and the Intensity of Anxiety* (Doctoral dissertation, Grand Canyon University).

Dictionary.com. (n.d.). Retrieved January 18, 2023, from https://www.dictionary.com

Freud, S. (2019). *The ego and the id*. Simon and Schuster.

Kirby, J. N., Tellegen, C. L., & Steindl, S. R. (2017). A meta-analysis of compassion-based interventions: Current state of knowledge and future directions. doi:10.1016/j.beth.2017.06.003

Lapsley, D. K., & Stey, P. C. (2011). Id, ego, and superego. *Encyclopedia of human behavior*, 1-9.

Luo, Y., Meng, R., Li, J., Liu, B., Cao, X., & Ge, W. (2019). Self-compassion may reduce anxiety and depression in nursing students: a pathway through perceived stress. Public Health, 174, 1-10. doi:10.1016/j. puhe.2019.05.015

McLeod, S. (2007). Maslow's hierarchy of needs. *Simply psychology*, 1(1-18).

McLeod, S. A. (2017, February 05). *Attachment theory*. Simply Psychology. www.simplypsychology.org/attachment.html

Neff, K. D. (2016). The self-compassion scale is a valid and theoretically coherent measure of self-compassion. Mindfulness, 7(1), 264-274. doi:10.1007/s12671-015-0479-3

Neff, K. D., Tóth-Király, I., Yarnell, L. M., Arimitsu, K., Castilho, P., Ghorbani, N., … Mantzios, M. (2019). Examining the factor structure of the Self-Compassion Scale in 20 diverse samples: Support for use of a total score and six subscale scores. Psychological Assessment, 31(1), 27-45. doi:10.1037/pas0000629

Puderbaugh, M., & Emmady, P. D. (2022). Neuroplasticity. In *StatPearls [Internet]*. StatPearls Publishing.

www.ingramcontent.com/pod-product-compliance
Lightning Source LLC
Chambersburg PA
CBHW031256250726
48655CB00005B/2240